More Praise for *Don't Forget to Flush*

"*Don't Forget to Flush* is the *Diary of a Wimpy k[...]* is simple and succinct yet full of humor and ir[...] a preteen in their spiritual growth. Preteens (a[...] find themselves going to the bathroom more c[...] reading! *Don't Forget to Flush* encourages pret[...] [...]ınd reflect on their faith as part of their daily rhythms and routines. And if a preteen can find God while they're going to the bathroom, they can probably find God anywhere and everywhere!"

Jim Keat, Associate Minister at The Riverside Church, product developer for Connect, *and founding member of FourFiveSix*

"Let's face it. Most devotional books for young teens are written so that only the most devoted Hermione Grangers of Sunday school would even consider picking them up. But *Don't Forget to Flush* puts inspiring, accessible, faith-building content in the very space where young people are guaranteed to be spending time each day. Easily digestible chapters, just the right amount of off-color, and a little silliness tucked into the bottom of each each make this the kind of book that even kids who "hate to read" just might pick up. I want to start giving this book to every confirmation student I know!"

Mark DeVries, Permissionary with Ministry Incubators, author of Sustainable Youth Ministry, *and founder of Ministry Architects*

"I've always said that parenting is so easy in the theoretical, and so hard in practice. That's why we all need this book! *Don't Forget to Flush* is both fun and formative. I think your kids will enjoy it, and I'm sure you'll love it. It promises to open up many conversations between you and your child about faith."

Andrew Root, Author of The Grace of Dogs: A Boy, a Black Lab, and Father's Search for the Canine Soul

"*Don't Forget to Flush* is a humorous and inviting introduction to a daily habit that will help kids connect the teachings of the Bible to the situations of their everyday lives. Whimsical drawings, stories, and thoughtful prompts delivered in the time it takes to visit the bathroom!"

Mark and Lisa Scandrette, authors of Belonging and Becoming: Creating a Thriving Family Culture *and* Free: Spending Your Time and Money on what Matters Most

DON'T FORGET TO FLUSH!

A BATHROOM DEVOTIONAL FOR KIDS

by Kevin and Britta Alton

◆

Illustrated by Graham Ross

SPARK
HOUSE
FAMILY
sparkhouse.org

Printed in the United States of America

23 22 21 20 19 18 17   1 2 3 4 5 6 7 8

ISBN: 9781506427010
Ebook ISBN: 9781506427027

Written by Kevin and Britta Alton
Illustrated by Graham Ross
Designed by Hillspring Books

Scripture taken from the Holy Bible, NEW INTERNATIONAL VERSION®, NIV® Copyright © 1973, 1978, 1984, 2011 by Biblica, Inc.® Used by permission. All rights reserved worldwide.

Library of Congress Cataloging-in-Publication Data
Names: Alton, Kevin, author.
Title: Don't forget to flush : a bathroom devotional for kids / by Kevin and Britta Alton ; illustrated by
    Graham Ross.
Description: First edition. | Minneapolis : Sparkhouse Family, 2017.
Identifiers: LCCN 2017025194 (print) | LCCN 2017033635 (ebook) | ISBN 9781506427027 (Ebook) |
    ISBN 9781506427010 (pbk. : alk. paper)
Subjects: LCSH: Christian children--Prayers and devotions--Juvenile literature. | Christian children--
    Religious life--Juvenile literature. | Etiquette for children and teenagers--Juvenile literature.
Classification: LCC BV4870 (ebook) | LCC BV4870 .A324 2017 (print) | DDC 242/.62--dc23
LC record available at https://lccn.loc.gov/2017025194

V63474; 9781506427010; AUG2017

Sparkhouse Family
510 Marquette Avenue
Minneapolis, MN 55402
sparkhouse.org

HOW TO READ THIS BOOK

STEP 1: Go into the bathroom.

STEP 2: Close the door (see chapter 1).

STEP 3: Read at least one chapter per bathroom visit.

STEP 4: Enjoy the fun facts and jokes along the bottom of the page.

STEP 5: Mark your place with a piece of toilet paper.

STEP 6: Don't forget to flush.

A MESSAGE FROM ELI

IF YOU HAPPEN TO BE READING THIS AT, SAY, YOUR KITCHEN TABLE OR ON YOUR BED, this would be a good time to let you know this is a *bathroom* devotional. Sure, it's in the title, but maybe you were in a hurry and just opened the book right up because it's your birthday or Christmas or something. Stop; take it to the bathroom and keep reading. I'll wait here.

I'm waiting. Seriously.

The idea is for this book to be your go-to (get it?) reading companion when you spend a little time in the throne room each day. You'll want to keep it in here. After all, this is where I did all the thinking for these stories anyway.

See, you and I both know that we *all* go to the bathroom *every* day. It's biology. Just like God intended. Even if God hadn't thought of it, *food* would probably insist on it anyway. That's why it occurred to me that the bathroom might be the perfect place to start a new daily habit—like attaching something I *want* to do to something I *have* to do. It's worked, too! Just the *click* of the bathroom door closing gets my mind popping with thoughts about God.

So I decided to share my top-secret method with a select group of friends we'll call "people who can read." Welcome to the club, dear reader. I figure if we get in the habit *now* of having some divine input on a daily basis, it can only be a good thing when you think of all the years of growing, being, and doing that we've got ahead of us.

I have a hard time remembering everything I'm supposed to do each day. I know that one of my chores is to take out the trash, but it's not until trash dumps all over the floor when I open the lid that I remember it actually needs to be done. I'm also supposed to take my dog, Muttley, for a walk, but sometimes I get sidetracked by building structurally questionable towers out of boxes and empty cans from the recycle bin. Luckily Mom always seems willing to give my memory a helping hand. She calls it a "brain nudge." But the point is this—you sometimes need a reminder to do the things that are important. Reading the Bible and figuring out how it applies to life right now is important. Learning to pray and finding out about how the people you love have grown in faith is super important. But it's also easy to get distracted, spending your day worrying over things like being on time, getting homework turned in, avoiding bullies in the hallway, and trying to be nice to your sister. Or whoever. Then all of the sudden you're lying in bed trying to fall asleep and realize that you never took any time out of the chaos for something called a "quiet time" in order to stay closer to God.

To be honest, the idea of quiet time *can* sound a little boring, and most of my stories aren't really quiet either. Good news: as you read, you don't even have to *try* to be quiet. It's *your* bathroom time after all. Be noisy. Make toot sounds. Talk to yourself. Sing a little. All that is totally cool here.

One last thought: you don't have to take my word for anything, especially about the Bible. You may see, hear, or feel something completely different. Totally fine. At some point I realized one of the best things about the Bible is talking about it with other people. I don't always understand what I read. You won't either—trust me, there's some weird stuff in there. I don't want to spoil anything if you haven't read it, so let's just say *not everybody lives*. If you read something confusing, find a grownup. Even when stories make sense, I've noticed that they hit me a little differently every time I read them. So don't be shy about sharing what you're thinking about the Bible—you just might show somebody something new, or they might share something new in return.

I'm afraid I've used up your entire bathroom visit without getting around to telling you a story. I just got excited when you opened the book because . . . well, it's dark in here with the cover closed. Don't worry about me, though. I'll see you soon enough.

And don't forget to flush.

— ELI

About the Authors

Kevin and Britta Alton have spent two decades advocating for and ministering to families and children of all ages. Kevin is a Christian ministry creative, collaborating in writing, editing, web development, and social media efforts all aimed at exploring and shaping the spiritual development of youth. Kevin is currently working on the Templeton grant project *Science for Youth Ministry* and is pursuing a masters of psychology at the University of Tennessee at Chattanooga. He has written, coauthored, and contributed to several books including, *The Whirl Story Bible, God's Graffiti Devotional, Faith Forward Volume 2*, and *SENT Youth Study Book*. Britta loves finding ways to assist, protect and build strong character through vocation or volunteerism. They live happily in the countryside with their two wonderful boys near Chattanooga, Tennessee.

About the Illustrator

A graduate of the illustration program at Sheridan College in Ontario, Canada, **Graham Ross** began his freelance illustration and design career in Ottawa. His career has spawned illustrations for publishers around the world, Canadian government agencies, and private design firms. He lives in Merrickville, Ontario, in a log cabin with his wife, Jenn.

SO THERE I WAS,
full of cheeseburger,
sitting on the toilet.
The porcelain throne.
The john. In my office,
so to speak, minding
my business. I was
trying to avoid my
mom's friends from
church who had taken
over the living room.
A full belly provided
the excuse for privacy.
I *like* going to the bath-

room. It's like a little vacay from the family unit. I can think in here. I
can read, like you're doing now. Sometimes I stay a little longer than I
need to just to have some alone time or rock out in front of the mirror.
Sometimes I talk to God. It's a great time to . . .

"Oh, I'M SO SORRY! I didn't realize you were in here, sweetie."

Oooooooohhh, bummer; I left the door open. Hope my mom's friend
wasn't totally traumatized. Quick, look: did you shut the door?

 IT'S POSSIBLE THAT AS MANY AS ONE BILLION PEOPLE IN THE
WORLD DO NOT HAVE A BATHROOM DOOR.

The door is important. In a moment of hurried weakness, I had failed to engage the primary protective agent of the restroom experience. The imaginary barrier between self and family unfortunately requires shutting an actual, physical door. I'm sorry, me, I have let you down.

Reminds me of a note my mom stuck in my backpack last week. It had Matthew 6:5-15 on it. You can read the whole thing when you get out of here, but this is the part that I just remembered:

"But whenever you pray, go into your room and shut the door and pray to your Father who is in secret; and your Father who sees in secret will reward you." (Matt. 6:6)

Going somewhere to be alone to pray helps me focus better on God. The bathroom is a great place for that. I don't always pray in here, but I should always shut the door. It's rule number one for number two.

Alright, you better get outta here. Ask a family member where they pray and what they like to pray about. And don't forget to flush!

YOUR TURN

- **What do you think about prayer?**
- **What do you pray when you pray alone?**
- **Do you have special places you like to pray sometimes?**

 Q: WHY SHOULD YOU ALWAYS REMEMBER TO FLUSH?
A: IT'S YOUR DOODY.

2

I BET YOU SHUT THE DOOR THIS TIME.

Getting walked in on last night was a little embarrassing, but it wasn't the first time that leaving the door open backfired. When I was younger, I used to wiggle my legs while sitting on the toilet. Once my pants dropped off my feet! I thought that was pretty funny until our dog, Muttley, trotted in, grabbed my pants, and took off.

"Man," I thought. "I'm gonna wish I had those in a minute."

Privacy is important, and not just for keeping your pants. Did you read the rest of the story in Matthew 6:5-15 I mentioned before? People sure have a bunch of different ways of praying. Some people like to pray for a *looooooonnnnnng* time and ask God to do a list of stuff. Others just seem to like the sound of their own voice. Maybe they're just nervous.

PRAYER IS MENTIONED OVER 600 TIMES IN THE BIBLE.

Jesus said in Matthew 6:5, *"And whenever you pray, do not be like the hypocrites; for they love to stand and pray in the synagogues and at the street corners, so that they may be seen by others. Truly I tell you, they have received their reward."*

When I pray alone, sometimes I don't even start with a name for God. God is already listening to me anyway—all the time. Not creepy listening. Just helpfully there. I like it. I don't think it matters *how* we pray, as long as we mean what we say.

But *listening* to God is just as important as what we *say* to God. The bathroom is a great place to find a little privacy for listening. You can't have a conversation if all you do is talk *at* somebody, right?

Why not take a moment and listen to the toilet flush before you go, huh?

YOUR TURN

- **What does it feel like when you listen during prayer?**
- **What helps you listen well?**
- **Ask a family member how they listen to God.**

 Q: WHAT CLOTHING ITEM DOES A DOG ALWAYS SEEM TO CARRY IN ITS MOUTH? A: PANTS.

3

I HAVE TWO USUAL BATHROOMS. Most times it's the one I share with Jasmin at home with Mom. But today it's the one Jasmin and I use when we go stay with Dad. He lives across town since he and mom divorced, but that's another story for another day. It's complicated.

Both bathrooms are good for being alone behind a closed door. Dad doesn't even mind if I lock the door so long as he doesn't hear any crashing or splashing sounds.

I went back and looked at that part in Matthew 6 about going into a room, closing the door and talking to God again. Verse 6 says, *"Close the door and pray to your Father, who is unseen."* And after the part about people babbling on with lots of words it says in verse 8, *"Do not be like them, for your Father knows what you need before you ask him."*

GRACIAS! MERCI! MAHALO! THAT'S "THANK YOU" IN SPANISH, FRENCH, AND HAWAIIAN.

When I came in the bathroom this morning, I realized I forgot my toothbrush. Before I could even wake up enough to wonder what to do, I saw a note on the back of the door that said, "Hey, buddy. I know you forget to pack stuff sometimes, so there's a brand new toothbrush in the cup on the counter for you, and I put out a towel in case you want to take a shower. I got you."

Kind of like my "Father, who is unseen," I don't see my dad every day, or my mom for that matter. But they know me better than anyone does. Better than I know myself. That's when I felt the huge light bulb pop on over my head. God knows me and what I need. Praying behind closed doors—like a private conversation—is still a good thing. But it can be about more than what I need in that moment. After all, God already knows what I need in that moment.

YOUR TURN

- **Who thinks of your needs before you even tell them?**
- **How does God provide for you?**

Go tell someone thanks for taking care of you. Right after you flush.

 A LIGHT BULB IS A SYMBOL OF A GOOD IDEA BECAUSE LIGHT BULBS WERE INVITED BY THOMAS EDISON—A MAN WITH MANY GOOD IDEAS!

4

IT DOESN'T SEEM TO MATTER how much superhero gear I wear, it's never enough for me to see in the dark! I've tried. I've got on my cape and my galoshes of invincibility. I even dug under my bed and found my super-spy night-vision goggles. Then I locked myself in the bathroom to try out my super-powered sight. I grabbed mom's verse-a-day calendar. No dice. It turns out they don't actually work—they just have green lenses. Now not only can I not see anything, but the corner of my cape is also wet.

If the goggles were real night vision, I wouldn't have tripped over the shoes I took off earlier and landed with my cape in the toilet. Good thing this was a tactical mission and not an actual bathroom visit! THAT would have been gross. So now I'm stuck using plain old light to read, but at least with my goggles everything is cool green.

NIGHT-VISION DEVICES OFTEN USE A GREEN TINT BECAUSE OUR EYES ARE MOST SENSITIVE TO GREEN LIGHT WAVELENGTHS.

"For God, who said, 'Let light shine out of darkness,' made his light shine in our hearts to give us the light of the knowledge of God's glory displayed in the face of Christ." —2 Corinthians 4:6

That's what started it all. When I saw that earlier, I imagined what it would be like to make light shine out of darkness the way God did. I should have gone for the flashlight. I mean ANYBODY can turn on a light switch. But to really go BAM and then make light happen? When I think of God doing that, I start to feel big and incredible—because God made me too! Maybe *I'm* a laser light, shining through the darkness. Only now with a slightly damp cape.

YOUR TURN

- **What do you see when you imagine making light shine out of darkness?**
- **If God's light shines in our hearts, what does that mean?**
- **Make the person who comes in after you feel super duper—don't forget to flush.**

 Q: HOW MANY CAPED CRUSADERS DOES IT TAKE TO CHANGE A LIGHT BULB?
A: NONE. THEY LIKE THE DARK.

5

I CAN'T SEE IN THE DARK. This was recently verified by my own scientific testing. And the power going out ten minutes ago. So I've decided to go in another direction. You may have noticed my bag. "Why," you ask me, "do you have such a heavy bag with you, Eli?"

"Aha!" I counter. "I think you'll find that this bag isn't heavy at all, but it is rather *light*!"

Here I use a dramatic swoopy dumping-out movement to reveal that all of the items in my bag create light. "*Voila!* I give you flashlight, minilantern, crummy promotional keychain light, bicycle safety light, and toy truck with operating headlights."

Why am I so wound up about light in the bathroom? It would be easy to point to a recent spy gear disaster, but the truth is the verses from

SOME FLUORESCENT LIGHT BULBS LAST MORE THAN TEN TIMES AS LONG AS INCANDESCENT LIGHTS.

2 Corinthians 4:1-7 have stuck with me. Verse 4 says, "*The god of this age has blinded the minds of unbelievers, so that they cannot see the light of the gospel that displays the glory of Christ, who is the image of God.*" My problem in here yesterday was not enough light. The problem facing Christians in 2 Corinthians was blinding light through the glory of Christ. What could be a better solution than *even more light*?

AHHH! TOO MUCH LIGHT! Just as I got all my little lights turned on the *actual* lights came back on, nearly blinding me. The first Christians reading 2 Corinthians didn't need *more* light. They needed *better* light. From a different source. I get that. There are a lot of "lights" shining into my life too—TV, internet, ads *everywhere*. Sometimes it's hard to fight through the noise to find anything meaningful.

Make one last noise before you go—don't forget to flush.

YOUR TURN

- If learning about God and love is one kind of light, what other lights fight for your attention?
- How do you decide what light to pay attention to?
- How is Jesus like a light?

11

Q: HOW MANY KIDS DOES IT TAKE TO CHANGE A LIGHT BULB?
A: ONE. USUALLY JUST THE ONE WHO BROKE THE LAMP.

6

IT'S WAY PAST THE TIME when I'm usually pretending to be asleep while reading under my blanket. It's even past the time when I pretend that I have to go to the bathroom one more time just to have an excuse to be up again. It's the time I always forget *exists*, because I'm ordinarily properly and soundly asleep.

But my upset stomach has been waking me up all night, so here I sit. I brought a book, but—welcome to my dilemma—I'm afraid to turn the light on. It's really, *really* dark, the kind of dark where you can kinda move around using just the tiny light shining from the smoke detector. I'm afraid that if I turn on the light my eyes will explode.

The inky darkness has me thinking again about those verses from 2 Corinthians 4:1-7. I think it's verse 6 that's standing out to me: *"for God, who said, 'Let light shine out of the darkness,' made his light*

THE DIMMER SWITCH WAS INVENTED IN 1959 BY JOSEPH A. SPIRA, USING A TAPPED AUTO-TRANSFORMER AND A DIODE. OBVIOUSLY.

shine in our hearts to give us the light of the knowledge of God's glory displayed in the face of Christ." Nothing like a little darkness to make that verse easy to imagine. All that light coming out of nowhere. It almost sounds alarming, but Jesus' light seems different. That light is supposed to come out of *me*. It's tricky, too. I'm not supposed to be *proud* of the light or try to use it as a superpower, which was my first thought. I'm supposed to show God to other people in my life, but be sure to point out that all the love and light is from God—not just me.

That was an awful lot to think about in the middle of the night. Oh, sweet! I just remembered: we have a dimmer switch here in the bathroom. Ahhh, just a *little* light.

Gross. Just enough light to remind me: don't forget to flush.

YOUR TURN

- **What do people learn about God from your life?**
- **If people think you're awesome or kind or even just nice to be around, how do you point their attention back to God?**

THE SUN'S MOM: BABY, YOU'RE THE BRIGHTEST THING IN THE GALAXY. WHY DON'T YOU WANT TO GO TO COLLEGE?
THE SUN: MOM, I'M GONNA BE A STAR.

7

"GO USE MOM'S BATHROOM! I'M THINKING!"

Sheesh. That's the third time my little sister, Jasmin, has come thumping on the door. It should be obvious by now that I am NOT coming out anytime soon. My legs went to sleep so long ago that if I stood up now I'd scream from the pins and needles. I decided to just let them sleep. I needed to do some serious thinking. Sometimes sitting here on the big white throne is the only place I *can* do it. I would say, "without being interrupted," but you'll probably hear more thumping any minute now—just ignore it. I do.

I tried to explain to Mom why I felt stressed. There's a huge science test tomorrow that I have to ace because I flunked last week's quiz. I'm supposed to be practicing lines for the school play. Next week I go up in front of the church and read a Bible verse. Betcha I flub up

 THE AVERAGE PERSON VISITS THE TOILET 2,500 TIMES A YEAR, SIX TO EIGHT TIMES A DAY.

pronouncing somebody's complicated name. If not that, something else will go wrong. And today at school we had a fire drill that had me thinking about scary stuff.

THUMP! THUMP! THUMP!

And now I get no peace. Sometimes it's all just *too much*. Mom tried to help by writing down a Bible verse: *"Do not worry about anything, but in everything by prayer and supplication with thanksgiving let your requests be made known to God." —Philippians 4:6*

ARE YOU KIDDING ME? *Do not worry*? Right. Like I can just get off the toilet with my numb legs and everything is supposed to be okay. I just don't know how to get from the first part of that verse to the second part. I'm going to give it a shot though and try out some of that prayer and supplication stuff. I'll let you know how it goes. Oh yeah—don't forget to flush!

YOUR TURN

- **What overwhelms you?**
- **What is the difference between worrying and praying?**
- **How do you think giving thanks can help you stop worrying?**

 IN AN AVERAGE LIFETIME WE SPEND THREE YEARS ON THE TOILET!

8

WHY DO I DO SO MUCH THINKING HERE?

Seriously. It's not like there aren't more comfortable chairs in the house. Pause and consider the toilet's construction. As you know, they're solidly constructed out of vitreous china—porcelain, in the common vernacular. It's a material uniquely suited to several jobs not generally described in devotional books. So I won't. The seat is the only place you could add some comfort, but for some reason most people—other than grandmothers—don't bother. "Get in and get out," was Dad's reply the one time I asked about getting an upgraded butt-rest.

Yet here I consider the meaning of life and all that I survey. It's . . . peaceful. It's an escape. Sure, sometimes I just sit here and laugh at my own noises. But sometimes I find myself thinking deeper stuff, too. I'm actually trying to make a habit of it. I mean, I've already got to be in here anyway. Might as well make an effort to connect with God.

SCIENTISTS WHO STUDY THE BRAIN HAVE FOUND THAT MEDITATION CAN INCREASE ATTENTION SPANS AND IMPROVE FOCUS.

The Bible talks about it in Philippians 4. It doesn't mention the bathroom specifically, but stay with me. Verse 6 talks about not being anxious, but verse 7 is more about what I'm feeling in here today: *"And the peace of God, which transcends all understanding, will guard your hearts and your minds in Christ Jesus."* There's a lot that goes on that transcends my understanding, but I like the sound of this kind of peace. I like to think about being surrounded by peace, especially God's peace. As an opposite example, your peace might be disrupted by your hectic schedule of homework and school and sports and even church activities. *Jasmin's* feeling of peace is easily disrupted by things like hiding her toys or changing the Wi-Fi password. Mom's peace too, on that one. But God's peace sounds so . . . unshakeable. Can't be moved. Solidly constructed, like vitreous china. I bet that's in a psalm somewhere.

It's also important to work out things like what snappy zinger you would have used in front of your friends if you hadn't walked into that locker. But spend some time in here thinking about how God loves you, too. Let's think about better things. Like being a better toilet flusher! Don't forget.

YOUR TURN

- **What do you think about most in the bathroom?**
- **Where do you feel God's peace the most?**
- **Ask somebody what makes *them* feel peaceful.**

SIR JOHN HARINGTON IS CREDITED WITH INVENTING THE MODERN FLUSHING TOILET. BEFORE HE WAS "SIR JOHN" THEY PROBABLY JUST CALLED HIM "THE JOHN."

9

I MAY HAVE UPSET THE NATURAL ORDER OF THE UNIVERSE.

I asked my mom if she could tell me some better things to think about when I think about things. She was already sitting down, which was probably a good thing. She started to answer, but her mouth just opened and closed.

Then she felt my forehead, as though she was checking for a fever. I thought I saw a tear forming in the corner of her eye, so I interrupted whatever was going on in her head.

"Mom?" I said.

"Just a minute, dear." She walked out of the room and came back a few minutes later with an index card with a stub of clear tape on it. "Put this wherever you like," she said.

 TOILETS DIDN'T ALWAYS HAVE WALLS AROUND THEM. ONCE THEY GAVE THEM WALLS, THEY CALLED IT A "WATER CLOSET."

Naturally I put it next to the toilet. Oh, boy. She'd given me a whole *list* of things to think about! I started reading it: "Whatever is true. Whatever is noble. Whatever is OH WAIT A MINUTE." I stopped reading. I finally recognized it; this was the *very next verse* from where I was reading in Philippians 4:8. *"Finally, brothers and sisters, whatever is true, whatever is noble, whatever is right, whatever is pure, whatever is lovely, whatever is admirable—if anything is excellent or praiseworthy— think about such things."* Good one, Mom. Sneaking God stuff into everything.

I found out later that the reason she reacted the way she did was because I'd done "something unexpectedly wonderful," which does sound like something Mom would like but also something I forget to shoot for most of the time. I guess I can work on that, too. Heck, I can meditate on it right now. Why don't you meditate on flushing before you head out.

YOUR TURN

- **What are the good things you like to think about?**
- **What *distracts* you from thinking about good things?**
- **What's something unexpectedly wonderful you can do for a family member?**

THEY SAY THE FLUSH "TONE" OF MOST TOILETS IN THE UNITED STATES IS IN THE MUSICAL KEY OF E FLAT.

10

DO YOU EVER READ IN THE BATHROOM?

Okay, dumb question—you're in the bathroom and this is a book. Point taken. How do you decide *what* to read? Do you go for laughs, or maybe try to read up on sports to have better things to say in the lunchroom at school?

I usually pick what I read, but one summer I spent a week at my Aunt Teresa's house. The first time I remember going to the bathroom at Aunt Teresa's I settled in, got adjusted on the seat just right, and looked for something to read. What? Nothing in here but a *dictionary*.

It was worse than I'd feared: *not* a dictionary. It was *Bible*. A Bible! In the bathroom! An outrage. The Bible seems like one of those things you just aren't supposed to touch while you're on the toilet. Like food. Or Jasmin's retainer.

 THE BIBLE IS ACTUALLY LIKE A LIBRARY—THERE ARE 66 SEPARATE BOOKS REPRESENTING ABOUT 1,500 YEARS OF HISTORY IN OUR BIBLE.

I wasn't sure I could do my business without reading *something*, so I grabbed the Bible and heaved it onto my lap. It was as heavy as a cinderblock. I flipped it open to Acts. Chapter 8, verse 26, actually. *"Now an angel of the Lord said to Philip, 'Go south to the road—the desert road—that goes down from Jerusalem to Gaza.'"* Angels. Cool. I kept reading. Philip runs into another guy without a name (it just says he's from Ethiopia) reading a copy of Isaiah. Suddenly I felt like I was in the story. *"Do you understand what you're reading?"* Philip asks in verse 30. The answer in 31: *"How can I unless someone explains it to me?"*

"I don't get it either!" I yelled. Everybody talks about how great the Bible is, but whenever I try to read it I bump into something weird or confusing. Who can explain it to *me*?

"ELI!" Aunt Teresa boomed. "Stop yelling and get out of there. And don't forget to flush."

"Maybe I'll ask her," I thought.

YOUR TURN

- When do you read the Bible? Do you try to read it like a regular book, or do you hunt for stories?
- It turns out questions about the Bible are a good thing—what questions do *you* already have about it?

Q: WHAT DID THE EARLY CHRISTIANS USE TO CHOP WOOD?
A: THE AX OF THE APOSTLES.

11

YOU KNOW, I think pretty often about that time at Aunt Teresa's when I got stuck in the bathroom with just her Bible to read. I can remember it like it was just yesterday . . . (Here's where it's helpful to imagine your vision going blurry and harp music playing as we go back in time to the scene.)

I did flush when she hollered at me. And thankfully I pulled my pants up before washing my hands, because just when I started washing them with the Bible laid open beside the sink, in walks Aunt Teresa. Like she owned the place. Which I guess she does. So, one point for her.

"What on earth are you yelling in here about, Eli?" She asked me.

 Q: WHAT IS THE BEST WAY TO START READING THE BIBLE?
A: YOU LUKE INTO IT.

I still had that story opened on the counter and told her I felt just like the guy in the story who didn't understand what he was reading. I saw a gleam in her eye that meant I was talking about something she really wanted to talk about. Next thing I know, she put the seat lid down for me on the toilet and sat herself down on the side of the tub. There was nothing to do but sit down with her and show her what I had found in Acts chapter 8. It was EXACTLY like the guy in the story with Philip.

I thought Aunt Teresa was going to giggle when she read verse 35. *"Then Philip began with that very passage of Scripture and told him the good news about Jesus."* I mean, I really thought she was going to hop up and do a little happy dance. She said, "It's like we're acting out this story, only in the *bathroom*!" She said that if I kept reading and trying to understand, and asking questions, that one day I could be the one other people asked for help when they got confused. Well, thanks for blowing my mind, Aunt Teresa.

YOUR TURN

- Who was the first person who told you about Jesus?
- Do you ever think of yourself as a person in a Bible story?
- When you leave here, go tell someone what you've been reading. Oh, but don't forget to flush first!

 THE COMPLETE BIBLE HAS BEEN TRANSLATED INTO OVER 500 LANGUAGES.

12

OH, FIDDLESTICKS.

I've made a terrible error. Reading my Bible in the bathroom has been working pretty well for me lately. Since Jasmin is playing at a friend's house, I was ready to settle in to the privacy chamber for a really long time. I made a plan. Bible? Check. Toilet paper? Check.

Door closed? Check. Then I followed proper seating procedure—lid up, pants down. Now I can . . . nooooooooo!

I look over the million miles between the sink counter and myself, and see that I left my Bible lying there. It's like the Grand Canyon of distance. You might think that it's a simple solution of getting up to go get it. But think again. You know how it goes. There's a point at which your body says, "Nope. We're doing this now." So here I am. Stuck. It reminds me of a verse I memorized in church once, Psalm 119:11: *"I have hidden your word in my heart that I might not sin against you."*

AT ITS WIDEST POINT, THE GRAND CANYON STRETCHES 18 MILES (29 KILOMETERS) ACROSS.

It might sound weird, but I memorized that one verse just as a reminder to myself to read the Bible more. Mrs. Johnson had challenged us to memorize a verse. If you're going to memorize just one, it might as well be one that reminds you to read more verses, right?

Sitting here now, it occurs to me that the more I can remember stories from the Bible the more it will be like always having reading material *inside* of me. A WHOLE BOOK INSIDE OF ME. Goals, people.

Of course, to get it inside me I'll have to do a better job of keeping the Bible on the same side of the room as me.

Well, be glad you've got your book, and don't forget to flush!

YOUR TURN

- **Besides this awesome book, what else could you keep in the bathroom to help build your faith?**
- **Are there other things besides books that you can read and get spiritual guidance from?**
- **Ask someone in your family if they read about God in the bathroom. If so, find out what they read.**

 THE STORY ABOUT PHILIP AND THE ETHIOPIAN IS ONE OF TEN STORIES IN ACTS ABOUT PEOPLE BECOMING FOLLOWERS OF JESUS.

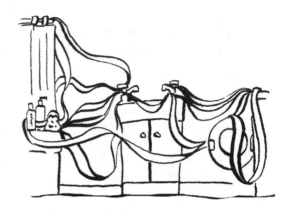

13

ONCE I MADE A LEGIT TOILET PAPER SPIDER WEB IN THE BATHROOM.

It was one of those things where you thought you had to go, but when you got to the bathroom you didn't really have to go yet and after a second you forget why you walked in there in the first place but then your brain thinks of something else and suddenly *that's* why you're there. I realize that was a long sentence, but that's kinda how it went in my head.

So I made a TP spider web. I started at the sink, because duh. Three times around the faucet, for strength. A quick toss over the shower rod through shampoo, conditioner, and a big poofy thing. Our washer and dryer are in our bathroom, and I used the lid of one and door of the other to complete my masterpiece.

ALARM! I *do* have to go.

I tore off the rest of the roll and hopped up on the toilet, replacing the roll on its holder. Crisis averted. When I was done, I reached for

THE AVERAGE ROLL OF TOILET PAPER HAS 500 SQUARES ON IT.

the TP and faced a new crisis: only two squares left, with half of one ruined with glue from the tube.

When I panic, I try to think of stories from the Bible. Not because I'm a spiritual know-it-all, but because it reminds me of the calming voice my Sunday school teacher, Mrs. Johnson, uses to read Bible stories. The story that came to mind has cows in it.

Pharaoh (basically the king of Egypt) had a dream about fat cows. During his awesome fat cow dream, some weird cows showed up. The weird cows *ate* the other cows. No seriously, check Genesis 41:20: *"The lean, ugly cows ate up the seven fat cows that came up first."*

The dream turned out to be about something else: not being wasteful. Joseph explained to Pharaoh that the awesome cows represented awesome times. After the awesome times came hard times.

If Pharaoh's dream had been about not building unnecessary TP spider webs, maybe I wouldn't be holding an empty tube. Hopefully I've saved you from getting in a tight spot of your own! Don't waste this opportunity to flush.

YOUR TURN

- **When have you been wasteful?**
- **How does being wasteful impact God's creation?**
- **How can you make a point of not being wasteful?**

 MY ROLL OF TOILET PAPER HAS ZERO SQUARES ON IT.

14

AFTER THINKING OF THE STORY FROM GENESIS 41 YESTERDAY, I went and read it again last night right before bed. That's got to be why I had such a crazy dream. In the dream I was sitting on my throne, just like you're doing right now. Minding my own

business. Doing my own business. That's when seven happy, puffy, adorably full toilet paper rolls came zip-lining down the shower curtain to land on the side of the tub. They were all dancing and laughing. I could hear the music. But just as my toe started to tap, I looked over and an empty toilet paper roll climbs out of my trash can and stands on the rim. It spots me and drops to the floor. While it rolls toward me, another empty roll climbs up and out of the can. One by one, seven empty toilet paper rolls roll over to my feet and then stand up staring at me grumpily. I thought they were going to say something, but then I heard Mom say, "Eli . . . it's time to wake up!"

DURING DREAMS, YOUR MIND IS LEARNING, SOLVING PROBLEMS, AND MAKING SENSE OF EVERYTHING YOU ABSORBED WHILE AWAKE.

Well . . . I can take a hint, God. When I came in here this morning, the first thing I did was make sure there was toilet paper on the roll. But then I also checked under the sink cabinet. I guess I might have freaked out a little if there had been seven rolls under there. Especially if they had started dancing. But there were three rolls. Right there in case I need them. Never to be wasted again in spider web building. I learned my lesson on that one.

In Genesis 41:31, Joseph told Pharaoh, *"The abundance in the land will not be remembered, because the famine that follows it will be so severe."* That was exactly how I felt when I was holding the empty tube after building the spider web. It was an awesome web, but it turned out to be a poor use of what I had.

Use a reasonable amount of TP, and don't forget to flush!

YOUR TURN

- **What kinds of things do you think it's wise to keep from running out of?**
- **Have you ever had a crazy dream? Do you think God could talk to you that way?**
- **Go ask someone you love if God has spoken to them in a dream.**

Q: WHY DID THE TOILET PAPER ROLL DOWN THE HILL?
A: TO GET TO THE BOTTOM!

15

I'VE BECOME QUITE AN EXPERT IN TOILET PAPER MANAGEMENT.
When I walk into the bathroom I do a quick check to make sure there's toilet paper on the roll and even some extras stocked up under the sink. And I never build toilet paper spider webs anymore.

I'm so good at it that I decided to help mom out. I started a little chart on the sticky note on the wall beside me. There's one in Mom's bathroom too. I decided that since my personal experience made me somewhat of an expert in this area, that I should use my gifts to the benefit of others. Kind of like Joseph used his ability to interpret dreams to help keep everyone from starving. When he explained the dreams to Pharaoh, he was put in charge of the whole land of Egypt. He collected food and stored it up in those seven good years. If you go and look at the end of Chapter 41 in Genesis, verse 56 says, *"When the famine had spread over the whole country, Joseph opened all the*

 MAY YOUR LIFE BE LIKE A DOUBLE ROLL OF TOILET PAPER. EXTRA LONG AND VERY USEFUL.

storehouses and sold grain to the Egyptians, for the famine was severe throughout Egypt."

Now, around here, I'm on constant TP patrol. If I see supplies getting low, I make sure it gets put on Mom's shopping list. I see it as my personal duty.

Heh, heh. I said *duty*.

Right now, according to my calculations it shows that in my bathroom here I currently have . . . Wait! There's a shortage. A toilet paper famine! Currently there are no rolls in reserve and only one-quarter of a roll left on the holder.

"MOM!" Gotta go fix this. Don't forget to flush!

YOUR TURN

- How do you think Joseph felt about being in charge of food supplies for so many?
- If you're the one keeping track of something, how does it make you more careful about how resources are used?
- Maybe you should go see if there's something as important as TP that you can watch over in your home.

 IN 1973, AMERICANS PANICKED BECAUSE OF EXAGGERATIONS ABOUT POSSIBLE TOILET PAPER SHORTAGES. STORES SOLD OUT, AND IT TOOK MONTHS BEFORE THE "CRISIS" WAS OVER.

16

"**GOD,** usually when I'm jumping right to asking for something in a prayer I kneel down, but right now there's a quarter-inch of water (and who knows what else) on the floor. My socks are shot, but I won't have to change pants if I don't kneel. Anyway, this time I *didn't do it*, God. Really, truly. I mean, you were watching, right? All I did was flush. I mean, I did what I did, then I flushed, but nothing broke household bathroom protocol. There was a gurgling noise, too much water, then my toes felt cold. From the ends of the earth I call to you, as my heart grows faint; lead me to the rock that is higher than I . . ."

Hold on. You missed the part at the beginning where I was yelling. Here comes Mom.

• • • • •

THE WEIRD KNOB NEAR THE FLOOR BEHIND YOUR TOILET SHUTS OFF THE WATER. KEEP TURNING TO THE RIGHT UNTIL IT STOPS.

Whew. Turns out I didn't need to freak out. There was a solution: a plunger, or what I used to call "the rubber hat with a two-foot stick." Mom showed me how to use it, so next time I'll be game-ready. Oh, and I scored Mom points! She heard that last part of my prayer. Mom keeps a little calendar in here that has some daily verses on it that I look at sometimes. Today's was from Psalm 61:1-3a: *"Hear my cry, O God; listen to my prayer. From the ends of the earth I call to you, as my heart grows faint; lead me to the rock that is higher than I. For you are my refuge."*

So what did I just learn? For one thing, moms like it when you quote Scripture—double points if you do it in a prayer. Also, God really is *with* us. Call out; don't freak out. The psalms, if you haven't noticed already, are a great place to go for comfort when you're in a panic. Well, you better split. Don't forget to flush . . . and maybe keep an eye on it after you do.

YOUR TURN

- **What makes you panic? How do you handle it?**
- **When has a bad situation prepared you for another problem later on?**

 THE WORD *PSALM* MEANS SONG. PSALMS INCLUDE A RANGE OF TOPICS: THANKFULNESS, RANTS, POETRY, SUFFERING, AND MORE.

17

PLUNGERS ARE STRANGE THINGS. I guess there is someone somewhere that could explain how they work, but to me it's really a mystery. I just know that in that terrible moment, when the water is overflowing (let's say it's just water), and your feet are getting wet, and life is turning into a pretty messy predicament, there is a great mystery that can help. Sound familiar? Mom would probably say I'm taking that a little too far.

It was funny how those verses worked in that intense moment of panic yesterday. Psalm 61:1 says, *"Hear my cry, O God; listen to my prayer."* Mom and I talked about it last night when I was getting ready for bed. I think she was so happy that I quoted Scripture and prayed at the same time that she thought I might be ready for some kind of upper-level God lesson. "You know Psalm 61 was a song that David sang when he was overwhelmed, too," she said. She laughed when I asked her if she thought David

IN THE TIME OF KING DAVID, PLUMBERS DEVELOPED A SYSTEM FOR CHANNELING WASTE WATER THAT HELPED CULTIVATE GARDENS.

had ever been overwhelmed by a toilet. It might not be as scary as Goliath, but it's pretty scary. When I lay down to go to sleep, though, I was really glad I got to talk through a moment of minor crisis with Mom.

I really *did* used to call the plunger a "rubber hat with a two-foot stick." Way back when I was just a kid, and long before I realized what a disgusting hat they would make. I never actually put one on my head. Nope. Not me. Never.

Well, don't you think it's time you flushed?

YOUR TURN

- **Have you ever used Scripture in a prayer?**
- **Can you think of a favorite verse that you could use in a prayer?**
- **Go ask someone if a plunger has ever made them think about God.**

 TO GET A BETTER SEAL, RUN THE PLUNGER UNDER HOT WATER TO SOFTEN THE RUBBER BEFORE USING. (GET AN ADULT TO HELP TOO!)

18

I AM CALM. I am so calm that a turtle sunning itself on a rock would look at me and think, "Why can't I be that chill?"

You see, I just walked into the bathroom a few minutes ago to find that the toilet was about to overflow. There is no way you can pin this one on me. But even though it's not my fault, I still walked right in. No dancing around and hooting and hollering from me this time. I stood there in front of the toilet and stared it down. Like it was an old Western movie and I was facing the guy in the black hat in the middle of the street. I *wanted* that toilet to overflow. Go ahead. I've got a plunger, and I'm not afraid to use it. Do you feel lucky, toilet? Do ya?

The other day I was feeling verse two from Psalm 61: *"I call as my heart grows faint; lead me to the rock that is higher than I."* But today,

ABRAHAM LINCOLN IS QUOTED AS SAYING, "I WILL PREPARE AND SOMEDAY MY CHANCE WILL COME."

I'm feeling verse three: *"For you have been my refuge, a strong tower against the foe."* I know this overflow is not the end of the world. Just like in life when I realize that God is with me in any other scary situation I face.

So I stood there ready, even eager, to use my newfound skills with the plunger. But right as the water got near the top, a couple of big bubbles gurgled up and then down went the water and the toilet made this funny gluckety sound as it did some kind of belated, slow motion flush. Thank you, Jesus. 'Cause I was willing, but really did not want to have to wrestle that beast today.

Now I can put this plunger away for another day. Hey you—don't forget to flush on your way out!

YOUR TURN

- **When was the last time you faced a scary situation?**
- **What would it feel like to have God standing beside you?**
- **Do you know how to use a plunger? If not, it's probably a good idea to ask someone.**

Q: WHAT DID THE PLUNGER SAY TO THE TOILET?
A: YOU LOOK A LITTLE FLUSHED.

19

LAST SUNDAY I HEARD THE MOST AWESOME STORY AT CHURCH.
Jesus said that it doesn't matter how dirty your hands are when you eat. I kid you not. I came home and looked it up and it is 100 percent there in my Bible! I owe my pastor big time for this.

Mom is going to call us for dinner soon, and I'm ready. I started on the bus ride home by licking my fingers real good. Then I touched the bus floor all around my seat. I dragged my hands down the rail as I got off, looked for worms and bugs under the big prickly bush that's by our back door and even hung on the tire swing for a while. I petted Muttley and even scratched his pits. Basically, I've touched everything I can think of. Holding them over the sink, I am stoked by the solid coating of grime an afternoon of hard work can gather. Even our car mechanic would be impressed.

THERE ARE MORE BACTERIA ON THE SKIN OF EACH HUMAN THAN THE ENTIRE POPULATION ON EARTH.

Here's the deal. There were these religious guys called Pharisees that kept trailing behind Jesus. It kind of seems like they were looking for mistakes they could gripe about. Their religious rules said, "wash your hands before you eat what's okay to eat." Some of Jesus' buds ate without washing up and of course the know-it-alls started pointing and shaking their heads. Then, in Mark 7:14-16, Jesus says to a crowd, *"Listen to me, everyone, and understand this. Nothing outside a person can defile them by going into them. Rather, it is what comes out of a person that defiles them."* Sassy and awesome.

I'll let you know how my experiment goes. I can't wait to see Mom's face.

YOUR TURN

- **Which do you think is cleaner right now—your hands or your heart?**
- **Wash your hands when you're done and imagine if it was that easy to make our hearts clean. (And don't forget to flush!)**

KNOCK, KNOCK. WHO'S THERE? VASHA. VASHA WHO? VASHA YOUR DIRTY HANDS!

20

I DON'T WANT TO SAY MY NON-HAND-WASHING EXPERIMENT WENT TERRIBLY, but the word does apply. Mom said she didn't want to dampen my first attempts at interpreting stories from the Bible. "I just want to dampen your hands with soap

and water!" Hilarious. Mom said I was missing the point of the story. And that if I didn't wash my hands, I'd be missing dinner.

Mom can be a real joke factory like that when she's making a point. I'm back in the bathroom now, washing my hands. Thoroughly. She even gave me a potato scrubber to get under my nails. I brought my Bible because a) this is going to take a while, and b) I have to figure out where I went wrong. Without getting my Bible wet.

After a quick read through Mark 7:1-19, I feel like I'm still right. I'll sum up: the disciples, our good guys, don't wash their hands. The Pharisees, the obvious antagonists (*not* good guys) in our story, waggle fingers and "Ahem!" their disapproval. Jesus, our hero, swoops in and (basically) says, "Dirty hands rule; handwashers drool." Game, set, match. What did I miss?

I can still smell Muttley-pit on my left hand, so I've got time for another once-over of the story. Hmmm. Is Mom calling me on a technicality? It doesn't actually say the disciples' hands were dirty. It says, "defiled," which I'll admit sounds even worse. Here, check out their question from Mark 7, verse 5: *"Why don't your disciples live according to the tradition of the elders instead of eating their food with defiled hands?"*

"Tradition of the elders" sounds a lot like, "Because I said so." Or, "that's just how we do it." Mom isn't like that though—she's not much on something being a rule just because it's always been a rule. It must be something else. I'll keep digging. In any case, I have to finish washing my hands for now. Don't forget to flush!

YOUR TURN

- **What do *you* think the Pharisees are really asking?**
- **What's most important to you about a story?**
- **What rule at your house would you like to know the reason behind?**

Q: WHY DID THE ROBBER WASH HIS HANDS?
A: HE WAS HOPING FOR A CLEAN GETAWAY.

21

JESUS MADE A POOP JOKE.

Well, maybe not a joke. And he didn't exactly say *poop*. But he totally mentions it, which is good enough. In fact, I wonder if he *did* make a poop joke and the writer was like, "Come on, Jesus. This is for posterity," before writing down Mark 7:18-19:

"'Are you so dull?' he asked. 'Don't you see that nothing that enters a person from the outside can defile them? For it doesn't go into their heart but into their stomach, and then out of the body.'"

Out of the body! Good one, Jesus. I see what you did there. Jesus is using a metaphor. While I'd have just used the metaphor to get away with making a poop joke, Jesus seems to be using it to get at something else. I don't always pay attention in science, but I do seem to remember that food doesn't go to your heart when you eat. Jesus appears to be up on his biology. So what he must be saying is that the things that can spoil us affect our heart, and . . . WOW. He doesn't mean our lub-dub heart. It's a metaphor stapled to another metaphor. Jesus is talking about our *inner* heart, the way-inside one that is kinda like the core of who we are. The one where we feel love for our grandparents, even if we forget to voluntarily hug them sometimes.

This just got a little heavy. Jesus isn't saying that everybody should get over hand washing. He's saying that we're worried about the wrong kind of keeping clean. If we get too focused on our outsides seeming super squeaky clean (like Christians sometimes try to do) we might forget to take care of our *insides*. I'll admit I was hoping for a dirty-hands permission slip from Jesus, but I think I may actually wash my hands more now. I can use it as a reminder about what I let get in to my heart.

Don't forget to flush!

YOUR TURN

- **When do you act like other people think you should?**
- **When do you disagree with people about how to act?**
- **What would you say is the most important thing about who you are?**

 IT TAKES BETWEEN SIX TO EIGHT HOURS FOR FOOD TO PASS COMPLETELY THROUGH YOUR BODY, DEPENDING UPON YOUR AGE AND GENDER.

22

EVERYONE KNOWS HOW TO FAKE BRUSHING YOUR TEETH.

It used to be so simple; all you had to do was do something cute and the question was forgotten. "Did you brush your teeth?" Giggle, followed by, "Mawma, I mades you a berfday cawd." That wasn't yesterday, for the record. I was maybe four at the time. But with each passing evening, the test

grew more difficult to pass. No longer did *cute* cut it. Even running the water for a few seconds didn't fool anybody. The moment you realize the dry bristles on your toothbrush are giving you away, they start checking your breath for minty-freshness. What's a kid to do?

It should be obvious by now that I don't always take the side of parents, but I need to give in on this one. First of all, I eventually realized

 DOG MOUTHS ARE *NOT CLEANER* THAN HUMAN MOUTHS, AS WAS LONG BELIEVED. UNLESS YOU KEEP FAKE-BRUSHING.

that it was actually more work to *fake*-brush my teeth than it was to actually *do* it. More importantly, I finally put together the look in my mom's eye when she realized I had faked it again with this verse my Sunday school teacher always calls "the golden rule," though I'm not sure what *that* means. Anyway, the golden rule is in Luke 6:31, and I bet you've already heard it: *"Do to others as you would have them do to you."*

I want Mom to always be honest with me, because I always want to know she means it when she says she loves me. I know she wants the same from me. And even if I can get away with something, I'm a better person when I'm honest.

Sorry to get all meaningful at the end. BOOGER BOOGER BOOGER! There, that should even things out. Don't fake-brush or fake-anything else. Be nice, and be honest. And don't forget to flush.

YOUR TURN

- **What are you regularly tempted to "fake it" about? Teeth? Shower? Homework?**

- **When are you *great* about being honest?**

- **Who—not just adults—sees the example you set about being honest?**

45

23

I'M AFRAID I'VE GOTTEN MYSELF INTO A LITTLE TROUBLE. It was all in the name of art.

It started innocently enough. After I had put toothpaste on my brush last night, there was a bug flying in front of me. When I swiped at it, there was a streak of toothpaste on the mirror. As I looked at it, I realized it looked like a mustache, and if I put my head just right, it fit right on me! Well, I felt inspired. Before I knew what I was doing, I reloaded my brush and went at it like I was Picasso. When I finally ran out of paint . . . . uh, toothpaste, I mean . . . I had managed to create a masterpiece that looked like some combination of Albert Einstein and Chewbacca. It was glorious!

I heard mom hollering at me to hurry up and finish brushing my teeth. That's where things went south. I looked down at my empty tube and realized I needed to borrow some from mom's bathroom. Well, I scurried around and got hers and dutifully started scrubbing. I only got a moment's warning before it all backfired on me. Just as I heard

Q: WHAT IS THE DENTIST'S FAVORITE MUSICAL INSTRUMENT?
A: A TUBA TOOTHPASTE.

her grumbling something about her toothpaste missing she knocked on the door and walked into my bathroom. (*Gasp.*) "ELI!!!!"

Gulp.

Remember the good old days when I was so responsible? If you'll recall, it was ME telling YOU last time about Luke 6:31: *"Do to others as you would have them do to you."* It's funny how one day and three ounces of toothpaste later, I'm suddenly needing a refresher course. Mom said that I would have plenty of time to remember it while I cleaned up my toothpaste mess. Much like saying or doing something you wish you hadn't, you can't just unsqueeze it back up into the tube. Sometimes you have to clean up the mess you made doing the wrong thing before you can move on to doing the right thing, I guess.

Well, don't forget to flush. And don't use all your toothpaste in artistic expression.

YOUR TURN

- **When was the last time you had to remind yourself about "the golden rule"?**

- **How do you want others to do unto you? How can you make that happen?**

- **Take a poll in your home to see who prefers Albert Einstein over Chewbacca. (The correct answer is Chewbacca, obviously.)**

 THE NAME "CHEWBACCA" WAS DERIVED FROM THE RUSSIAN WORD SOBAKA, MEANING "DOG."

24

A LITTLE WHILE AGO

I was sitting here with my pants around my ankles, and the perfect opportunity to practice the golden rule nosed through the door. Muttley came in for a little pat on the head because I didn't push the door all the way closed. When I leaned down, he tried to

sneak in a face lick, but his breath just about knocked me out. "Whoa, Muttley! Your *breath* smells like *death*, boy! Let's fix it."

I finished up job number one (well, number two, technically speaking) then hopped up to grab my toothbrush and my brand new tube of toothpaste. At first Muttley was excited. I guess he thought it was a special treat. I managed to get a couple of his big front teeth before his mouth became a rapidly moving target. I could tell I got some toothpaste in there though, because he started tossing his head around and sneezing like a really irritated rabbit. If I hadn't just finished going to the bathroom, I'm pretty sure I would have wet my pants laughing.

A LITTLE SPRINKLE OF CINNAMON OR A TEASPOON OF COCONUT OIL ON YOUR DOG'S FOOD WILL HELP CURE STINKY DOG BREATH.

Mom walked in the door and Muttley went scampering out so fast he almost knocked her over. She looked at me holding the toothbrush in one hand and the toothpaste in the other and the trail of minty fresh dog slobber that trailed out the door behind Muttley. She knew the whole story in a glance.

I gulped and said, "Luke 6:31, Mom. *'Do to others as you would have them do to you.'*" I could see her mouth twitch to the side as she calculated my use of Scripture against the trail of minty mess. Somehow humor won as she smiled and said, "I guess Muttley gets to brush your teeth tomorrow?" She took the toothbrush from me and put a scrubby sponge in my hand and kissed me on top of the head. "And you're lucky I bought you a new toothbrush to go with that tube of toothpaste. Let's let the vet brush Muttley's teeth from now on." I get it.

Hey—you better flush and get out of here!

YOUR TURN

- **Have you ever tried to do something nice and then have it backfire on you?**
- **Do you pray for guidance before you try to do something helpful? (It's not a bad idea.)**
- **Go and ask a parent for tips about some helpful ways to "do to others" around your house.**

49

 Q: WHAT IS A DOG THAT SNEEZES?
A: ACHOOWAWA!

25

IT WAS NEVER MY INTENTION to end up upside-down in a creek, but here I am drying off after a dunk.

It came about because yesterday I washed my hands just like I'm supposed to. Mom was thrilled to find a "teachable moment" when I accidentally left the hand towel on the floor after drying them off. It was careless, I admit. But Mom seemed especially disappointed sounding as she said, "I just want you to appreciate when things are provided for you. Not just by people, but by God too." She suggested that I do some searching for stories about God's provision.

After some thinking time in my room, I came up with a doozy. In 1 Kings 17, God provided for Elijah in a really cool way. According to verse 4, the Lord said, *"You will drink from the brook, and I have directed the ravens to supply you with food there."* So while birds brought him bread and meat each morning and evening, Elijah got water from a brook. It sounds pretty simple as long as you're cool

RAVENS ARE GREAT AT MIMICKING SOUNDS. THEY CAN MAKE SOUNDS LIKE HUMAN VOICES, CAR ENGINES, OR EVEN FLUSHING TOILETS!

with the fact that God organizes wild stuff like that all the time. And it fit right in with what Mom was trying to get through my skull.

Where it went wrong was my curiosity about drinking from a brook like Elijah did. I had to try it. Elijah's brook must have had some kind of perfect bank where he could kneel and drink. Mine does not. Which is why I'm standing here drying off. Elijah needed the water; Eli just needed a towel. I'm going to go explain to Mom how thankful I am that God sends ravens. And moms.

Don't forget to flush!

YOUR TURN

- **When have you ever tried to experience something you read in a Bible story?**
- **When can you remember God providing for you?**
- **Ask someone you love what God has provided for them.**

THERE ARE ABOUT 30 DIFFERENT TYPES OF BIRDS MENTIONED IN THE BIBLE. THEY DON'T ALL SERVE FOOD, HOWEVER.

26

I TOTALLY FORGOT TO BE THANKFUL. Mom sent me to the bathroom to take what she called a "much-needed shower," whatever that means, and she added the caution, "keep an eye out for the provisions." Veiled in mystery, she is. Wait, what's this? A note on the door! Notes. Maybe this is what she meant by "provisions." *"Leave here, turn eastward*

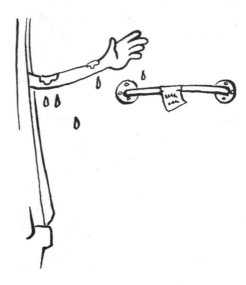

and hide in the Kerith Ravine, east of the Jordan" (1 Kings 17:3). Nope. A mystery was afoot.

When I came into the bathroom, there was *another* note on the shower door. "Kerith Ravine," it said. Ah HA. Mom was being goofy again. This was from the Elijah and ravens story from 1 Kings 17:1-6. God told Elijah to go hide in the ravine. Sometimes Mom doesn't make any sense.

So I took my shower without thinking about it anymore. Or at least until I was finished. I opened the door and reached for my towel.

Hmmm. Instead of a towel, my dripping hand found another note on the towel rod. "RAVENS BUSY, BRB." Be right back? What on earth does that have to do with where my towel . . . oh, right. *Provision*. Mom is the ravens, I am the Elijah. For some reason the shower is a ravine, but I don't think that's as important in what Mom is trying to point out.

I dribbled over to the bathroom door. "Mom?" I called out. "Need something, dear?" she asked. "Do we have any clean towels?" I asked, because it was what she wanted. We always have towels, thanks to Mom, but sometimes it's good to play along with the lesson. "Nevermore," Mom said.

"What?"

"Nothing. I'll bring you one in a moment. Why don't you hop back in the ravine so you don't make a pond of yourself in the floor."

Mom may have a strange way of making a point sometimes, but I think I'll remember to be thankful for provision from now on. Hey, make somebody else thankful and don't forget to flush.

YOUR TURN

- Who makes sure you have clean towels at your home?
- When have you realized that you were taking something for granted?
- How do you show gratitude for provision in your life?

53

 "THE RAVEN" IS A FAMOUS POEM BY EDGAR ALLAN POE.

27

MOM DOESN'T THINK I'M UNGRATEFUL, but I know that sometimes I forget to notice that my world doesn't magically appear around me, meeting my every need on its own. My clothes don't fold themselves. The toaster pastries aren't an unlimited resource. And the towels are hung for

me with care. When I'm here, Mom makes all of that happen. Dad does it at Dad's. The world—according to both of my parents and several posters of the universe I've seen at school—*doesn't* actually revolve around me.

I think the fact that I'm not the center of the universe actually makes the idea of provision even more special. I mean, if it were just *supposed* to happen, where would the love be? At the end of the story in 1 Kings 17 about Elijah, we get to see some of God's love in verse 6:

 IF YOU GO LOOKING FOR THE CENTER OF THE UNIVERSE, IT COULD TAKE A WHILE: SOME SCIENTISTS SAY THERE *ISN'T* ONE.

"the ravens brought him bread and meat in the morning and bread and meat in the evening, and he drank from the brook."

See? God apparently even noticed that Elijah was a big fan of sandwiches. If I'd been Elijah, God would have sent the ravens with cereal and cheese sticks. Oh, and probably some cookies. One big difference between me and Elijah is that he seems to be a drip-dry dude; the Bible doesn't say anything here about ravens bringing towels. Mom knows that I can't stand to drip dry. It takes too long. Plus there's a lot of confusion about whether I'm hot or cold.

I'm definitely cold until I'm dry, so I've decided to crank up my gratitude for the towels in advance. This morning I left a note thanking the ravens—er, Mom—for providing a way for me to dry off when I'm clean.

YOUR TURN

- **What's a new, creative way you can thank someone for providing for you?**
- **What are some ways people provide for you?**
- **Did you remember to flush?**

 THE ONLY PERSON THE BIBLE EVER MENTIONS HAVING A TOWEL IS JESUS.

28

I GOT CAUGHT HAMMING IT UP IN THE MIRROR AGAIN.

Showing off. Playing supermodel. Hair gel? Check. Clean teeth? Check. Snazzy shirt? Check. I just can't help it if sometimes I just look so good that I can't seem to stop looking. Even Jasmin stopped to stare on her way to

find Muttley. But when *Mom* catches me as I lean back, waggle my eyebrows, snap my fingers and point at myself, I suddenly feel silly even though nothing changed about how good I look.

Why did I suddenly feel silly? Good question. I thought about it for a long time, while staring at myself in the mirror. Hair gel is still holding my hair in a perfect swoop. No food caught in my teeth. My favorite shirt is still super cool. Then Mom walked back to the door and gave me that goofy look that only a mom can give you, like somehow I'm the best thing she can imagine. I felt my face turn pink as she kissed my forehead and slipped a note in my hand.

MIRRORS WERE FIRST MADE OUT OF POLISHED STONE, BUT THE ROMANS MADE THE FIRST GLASS MIRROR NEAR THE TIME OF JESUS.

"The Lord does not look at the things people look at. People look at the outward appearance, but the Lord looks at the heart." —1 Samuel 16:7b

It was kind of like reading something out of a fortune cookie, except the opposite. Like the reverse of "A new wardrobe will bring you great joy," which I got the other night at dinner. Where does Mom find this stuff? Sometimes I think God put the Bible together just for me to learn lessons from. I'm not sure I'm a fan of this verse. It kind of puts my looking good to waste. I guess I'll have to read some more of that story so I can understand.

Don't forget to flush!

YOUR TURN

- **What do you think it means by saying the Lord looks at your heart?**
- **If there was something in your heart that you didn't think God would like, what would you do about it?**
- **Spend time looking at a family member. What clues does their appearance give about what is in their heart?**

 Q: WHAT DID ONE MIRROR SAY TO THE OTHER MIRROR?
A: I SEE A LOT OF YOU IN ME.

29

I'VE BEEN IN HERE A WHILE NOW. I've been working. I can't get past 1 Samuel 16:7; it's stuck in my head. Why wouldn't it matter what somebody looks like? And what in the world is God looking at that we're not?

I brought a dry erase marker with me this time so I could try to look at myself from different angles. I traced myself in the mirror, hoping to stand off to the side and try to see whatever it is that God might be looking for *in me*, but I realized I'm just looking at the *outside* again. Like Samuel.

In the story from 1 Samuel 16, Samuel is there to pick out a new king. I assume Samuel is a pretty smart dude. They did name two books of the Bible after him. In verse 1 of chapter 16, God gives him a job:

Q: WHY DO MIRRORS LIKE TO HANG OUT AROUND A CAMPFIRE?
A: A LITTLE TIME FOR REFLECTION IS ALWAYS GOOD.

". . . Fill your horn with oil and be on your way; I am sending you to Jesse of Bethlehem. I have chosen one of his sons to be king."

So Samuel goes to see Jesse, expecting to find something kingly looking to anoint. Behold, the oldest son Eliab! Perfect. But no. God says to ignore his appearance and his height. I wish God had been at basketball tryouts—I could have used some of that kind of support.

What is God looking at if God isn't looking at my magnificent outside? My magnificent *insides*? That would be like . . . . like God, now that I think about it.

Everything eventually seems to be pretty simple with God. I just have to relearn how to look at everything.

YOUR TURN

- **What's your favorite thing about how you look?**
- **What about your *inside* self does God think is pretty great?**
- **Don't forget to flush!**

 THEY SAY YOU SHOULDN'T SPEND THE WHOLE DAY IN FRONT OF THE MIRROR, BUT I CAN TOTALLY SEE MYSELF DOING IT.

30

I'M SUPPOSED TO BE GETTING READY FOR SCHOOL, but I just can't figure out what I want to wear. Nothing special is happening. It's just Wednesday. But I've tried on nine different shirts, and all nine of them are on the floor, because they just weren't . . . right, I guess. I put them on, looked in the bathroom mirror, said, "Nopey-noperson," and threw them down.

In a minute or two, Mom is going to come in and remind me that I actually picked out *all* of these shirts when we bought them. I've worn them all, too. I've probably got at least three really happy memories attached to each. But I just can't figure out which one is right for *today*.

 A TYPICAL FAMILY OF FOUR CREATES NEARLY TEN LOADS OF LAUNDRY PER WEEK.

I finished reading that story last night in 1 Samuel 16 about Samuel trying to pick a new king. It was sort of the same deal—there wasn't anything *wrong* with Eliab or Abinadab or Shammah or the rest. Probably good-looking guys of various sizes. But God had something specific in mind. Like me, looking for a shirt.

In verse 12, this kid David gets brought in. He's the youngest son. The Bible says, *"He was glowing with health and had a fine appearance and handsome features. Then the LORD said, 'Rise and anoint him; this is the one.'"* Totally unexpected.

So it isn't *wrong* to be good looking—I'm just not supposed to make it the most *important* thing. OH SWEET! Mom just opened the door a little and stuck her hand in holding my favorite shirt. Whenever it's clean, it's the first one I set out to wear. I better get the rest of these back in my closet.

YOUR TURN

- **What does God see in you that is good?**
- **How can you take care of your appearance without it becoming the most important thing?**
- **Don't forget to flush!**

 A TYPICAL DAY AT DISNEY WORLD CREATES NEARLY 300,000 POUNDS OF LAUNDRY A DAY. ONE MORE WAY YOUR HOUSE ISN'T DISNEY WORLD.

31

I'M GOING TO TEACH YOU AN EXPERIMENT.

(It's also a way to measure growth.)

The question is, "What does *that* weigh, plus *me*?" You need yourself, a scale, and one other thing. The boring way to find out the answer is to weigh an object on the scale and add that number to your weight. If you're like me, you already know what you weigh dressed, dressed with shoes, undressed, and even with *just* shoes on. The *fun* way to do it is to pick up the item and weigh both of you at the same time. What do all the towels plus you weigh? What about with all the magazines?

I started paying attention to our scale when a basketball coach told me that I wasn't big enough to play. But the truth is, I've been growing my whole life. I've only documented the last few years, but they tell

 BEFORE MY LEGS GREW LONGER, I WASN'T ALWAYS THE FIRST ONE TO CLASS. BUT I'D BE THERE SHORTLY.

me I'm "a work in progress." Do they just mean size? We don't know what Jesus weighed, but Luke 2:40 says that he was growing too: *"The child grew and became strong; he was filled with wisdom, and the grace of God was upon him."* Luke 2 is a big deal, if you haven't read it. Angels talk about Jesus; he gets declared the Messiah—stuff like that. Then after this verse Jesus runs away for a minute. Normal.

Growing in size isn't the only measurement of maturity, and it sure isn't a measure of our worth. I don't think angels told my parents how I'm going to turn out. At least Mom and Dad haven't mentioned it. I'm still growing though, just like Jesus. I wonder how he kept track? Marks on the door frame above his head? Scales can't measure *wisdom*. I know I'm less nervous about praying out loud than I used to be. A lot of Bible stories sound familiar now. I guess I'm growing in wisdom too! Keeping track of how big you are and what you and the dog weigh with a scale is great, but there's other growth that's pretty important too.

Another way to measure things is time, which reminds me: you better go. No, I mean *leave*. Don't forget to flush!

YOUR TURN

- **What's something you specifically remember finding out about God?**
- **Who do you look up to for their faith? How can they help you grow in yours?**

 A STONE CAN BE A UNIT OF MEASURE, WITH ONE STONE BEING EQUAL TO ABOUT 14 POUNDS. HOW MANY STONES DO YOU WEIGH?

32

I NOW WEIGH EXACTLY 63 POUNDS MORE than I weighed when I was born. It's taken me a long time. Not because I haven't been trying. Mom says I have a hollow leg, and when we have chicken tenders for dinner I can go back for seconds or even thirds if nobody stops me. Sorry about that, chickens.

Last night was another one of those nights when Mom's friends come over and talk about who knows what. I was hiding from the cheek-pinchers when I heard a lady shrieking followed by my mom saying, "I know! Wasn't he the most adorable little thing?" And then I heard her telling them about all kinds of dumb things that I've said or done. You know—back when I was a little kid. I was mortified. I'm pretty sure I went to bed before 7:00 p.m. just so I didn't have to hear how cute I was anymore.

Q: HOW ARE FISH AND BATHROOMS THE SAME?
A: THEY BOTH HAVE SCALES!

That's why today I've been in here weighing myself. I'm trying to remind myself how big I am. That I'm not a dumpling-faced, fuzzy-headed baby anymore. Luke 2:40 talks about Jesus growing and being filled with wisdom, and all that was before he was 12! In the next few verses, Jesus gets separated from his family. When they searched, they found him in Jerusalem listening to the teachers in the temple—and they were listening to him!

After the chaos of the search, it says in verse 51, *"Then he went down to Nazareth with them and was obedient to them. But his mother treasured all these things in her heart."* I guess that's what my mom was doing last night. Just "treasuring" me in her heart even though (maybe because?) I keep growing. Just wish it didn't have to be so embarrassing.

Speaking of embarrassing—it sure would be if you forgot to flush!

- **How old do you think you have to be before you do things that teach others about faith?**
- **What kinds of things do you do that might be "treasured up" by someone who loves you?**
- **Who loves to tell stories about your growing years? Go ask them to tell you one of their favorite memories.**

 ALL SCALES MEASURE WEIGHT WITH MECHANICAL PARTS, SO WHETHER A SCALE IS MECHANICAL OR DIGITAL, IT IS ONLY THE DISPLAY THAT DIFFERS.

33

HOW'S IT COMING ALONG THERE FOR YOU? I mean in life. Not like *right there* and *right now*. That would be gross. Plus, I'm sure you can take care of that all by yourself. What I mean is how is your progress in this thing called life?

I've been picturing myself at different stages in my life. When I was a doofy toddler, I couldn't even make the scale turn on for me. And as I've grown, my parents have marked my height on different door frames to keep track. Today, if I stand on a stool or a stack of books, I can almost be as tall as my dad. Sometimes I try to imagine if I had grown that much already. Crazy.

Q: WHAT IS ONLY A SMALL BOX BUT CAN WEIGH OVER A HUNDRED POUNDS? A: A SCALE.

It's made me think about Luke 2 again. In the last verse of that chapter about Jesus growing, verse 52 says, *"And Jesus grew in wisdom and stature, and in favor with God and man."* I was thinking how cool it would sound if it read, "And *Eli* grew in wisdom and stature, and in favor with God and man." You can see how it sounds with your name too.

Then I started imagining what it would be like when I was bigger, older, smarter, and even more awesome than I am now. I don't really have to try to grow in stature. That kind of happens by itself. But if I keep trying, I'll get tons more wisdom as I learn. And if I use what I learn well, then I'll please God. Of course, you can't fake that kind of growth. I mean, I can't just jump on the wisdom scale and say it adds up to more. I've got to actually get there. So do you!

Well, when you get done, don't forget to flush!

YOUR TURN

- **If you had to step onto a wisdom scale right now, what do you think you would see about yourself?**
- **How do you think wisdom helps us grow in favor with God and others?**
- **Go write Luke 2:52 using your name in the verse and then post it where you can see it.**

 HUMAN GROWTH SPURTS ARE CALLED "PEAK GROWTH VELOCITY," AND AROUND THE WORLD THEY DO NOT ALWAYS HAPPEN AT THE SAME AGE.

COMMUNITY

34

LATELY, JASMIN AND I HAVE BEEN HAVING A HARD TIME sharing the bathroom. Not like "at the same time" kind of share. More like "get out so I can get in" kind of share. Last night it got pretty awful. I really had to GO! Jasmin was in here washing off her retainer before she went to bed. She washed and washed and washed. That thing had to be so clean we could have used it to whisk eggs. Sorry. That's too gross.

Anyway—it was clean enough. Meanwhile, there I was doing the pee-pee dance in the hallway. When I started hollering through the door about where I was going to throw that retainer when I got hold of it, Mom came and stopped me with one of her looks. That kind of mad, kind of sad look that means she's going to pray for me. She did.

This morning, she called us both in here to have a family bathroom meeting. Wouldn't you know there was something in the Bible about

Q: WHAT DID THE MAMA BEAR SAY TO THE BABY BEAR WHEN HE WET HIS PANTS? A: URINE BIG TROUBLE!

this? She read to us from Matthew 7:7-8. It says, *"Ask and it will be given to you; seek and you will find; knock and the door will be opened to you. For everyone who asks receives; the one who seeks finds; and to the one who knocks, the door will be opened."*

Mom said she was praying for us to respond with care when we hear a knock, and when we're the one knocking, that we would knock with respect. "What about when it's an emergency like last night?" I asked. After a long look at me, she said, "I'm sure you'll figure out something if you just think about it."

Secret code knocks! It popped in my head so fast I figured it had to be a message from God. Jasmin and I got started on a Bathroom Emergency Knocking Plan right then and there. I wasn't sure if that's what Mom had been aiming for, but she left us to plot. Wouldn't it be funny to have a secret code for talking to God? Beep boop boop bing—that's secret code for "don't forget to flush."

YOUR TURN

- How do you feel when someone ignores you when you have an urgent need?
- Have you ever prayed about a problem and found a solution in the Bible?
- Hey! After you flush (don't forget), go stand on either side of your bathroom door and think how it feels to be on each side.

71

THERE ARE EXERCISES YOU CAN DO TO HELP "HOLD IT." YOU CAN CONTRACT THE MUSCLES THAT STOP THE FLOW TO TRAIN YOUR BLADDER TO WAIT.

35

**TAPPITY-TAPPITY-
TAP-TAP.** Nope.
*Tappity-tap-tap-
THUMP.* Hmmm . . .

I'm practicing some
new knocks. Jas and I
have agreed, in prin-
ciple, to some code
knocks. Since we last
spoke, I have devel-
oped an elaborate
system of 16 knocks,
indicating why the bathroom is needed and how urgently. The third
section of knocks covers . . .

BAM!

"Who is it?"

"It's Jasmin. That's your warning knock. Two knocks means I'm going
to tell Mom."

KNOCK, KNOCK. WHO'S THERE? NOBODY. NOBODY WHO?
(SILENCE)

Her plan is a little oversimplified, but I see her point. Mom told us the other day that she wasn't as worried about how we knocked as much as that we started being more considerate to each other. In fairness, we've been pretty *inconsiderate* at times—lots of yelling about not a lot. Mom gave us a couple more verses to think about at breakfast the next morning. Philippians 2:3-4: *"Do nothing out of selfish ambition or vain conceit. Rather, in humility value others above yourselves, not looking to your own interests, but to the interests of the others."*

If we're going to learn to be more considerate to each other, I suppose the door is a good place to start. I mean, if the door were just for yelling through, you probably wouldn't need a door. Maybe the door just reminds us that we're supposed to be considerate on both sides of it. Speaking of being considerate: don't forget to flush.

YOUR TURN

- **How do you feel when someone is especially considerate to you? Or when you're considerate to someone else?**

- **When have you had a hard time remembering to be considerate? Why is that hard sometimes?**

Q: WHEN IS A DOOR NOT A DOOR?
A: WHEN IT'S AJAR.

36

I HAD A PRETTY GOOD GUESS what "selfish ambition" meant in Philippians, but I had to look up *vain* and *conceit* separately. Used together, Mom was suggesting that we needed to avoid pride in thinking we're more awesome than everybody. That's hard for me, honestly. I mean, check me out:

awesome. Whatever happened to looking out for my self-esteem?

Mom said she might have overshot with that verse, so she wrote *another* Bible verse about it on the door for us to read on the way in. It's right next to the other one, in Philippians 2:5: *"In your relationships with one another, have the same mindset as Christ Jesus."* Oh, be like Jesus. Never heard that one before, Mom.

So I closed the door like usual, but now I'm sitting here and suddenly wondering something very, very important: what was Jesus' mindset in the bathroom? I don't mean what did he *do*, I mean what did he think about?

Somewhere between Jasmin's first and second knocks it occurred to me. Jesus probably spent his time thinking about the people on the other side of the door. In the stories I've read, Jesus was surrounded by people most of the time. A lot of those people loved and respected him, but a lot just made trouble too. I bet he used his alone time to talk to God about how to be kind to everybody.

I bet he was quick in here too. If you're really into being considerate to the people around you, you should probably be quick on the pot. I'm going to try to keep that in mind from now on. Wanna give it a try with me?

Oh, speaking of being considerate to the people on the other side of the door—don't forget to flush.

YOUR TURN

- **Where else do you find space to spend some quiet time with God?**
- **How can you make sure that you're offering (or at least not interrupting) that kind of space for others?**
- **Who is on the "other side" in other parts of life that you can be more caring toward?**

 A DOOR WITHOUT HINGES IS JUST A WALL.

37

DON'T FORGET, DON'T FORGET, DON'T FORGET, DON'T FORGET.

I know you're thinking, "to flush," because I say that a lot and it's the title of the book you're reading. Don't be so suggestible. What I'm trying to remember is . . . nuts. It's gone. Oh wait—I'm trying to remember to *turn off the lights*. Not this moment. When I leave.

I have this habit. Mom calls it a "bad habit." It's actually not even something I *do* so much as it is something I *don't do*—I don't turn off the lights. All the time and anywhere I go, if I'm being honest. I just don't think past . . . right now, really. Past my own immediate needs. I need light when I come into the bathroom; it doesn't occur to me that I *do not need* light after I leave. I tried to tell Mom I'm just trying to be the light of Jesus in this world, but she wasn't having it. She even went so far as to tell me to leave Jesus out of my excuses. She also pointed out that we pay a bill for the lights, and we only get charged

Q: HOW MANY KIDS DOES IT TAKE TO CHANGE A LIGHT BULB?
A: NONE. USUALLY KIDS AREN'T ALLOWED TO TOUCH LIGHT BULBS.

for when they're *on*. Who knew? Conservation works at the family level, too.

I should tell her to leave the Bible out of her clever parental retorts, but I think they're pretty funny most of the time. Example: When I came into the bathroom a minute ago, there were three sticky notes on the light switch. The one above it said, "Day." The one below it said, "Night." The middle one read, "The light switch is God—Genesis 1:3–5."

When I was done I hurried to get my Bible, then doubled back to the bathroom because I forgot to turn off the light. I switched it off and then switched it on again because it was too dark to read. (See my problem?) *"God saw that the light was good, and he separated the light from the darkness"* (Genesis 1:4). I get it, Mom. God is like the light switch.

Be like God! Separate the light from darkness. And don't forget to flush.

YOUR TURN

- **Why does turning off the lights in a room when you leave matter?**
- **Which light are you most likely to leave on?**
- **Why is conserving electricity something Christians should care about?**

 LED LIGHT BULBS ARE BEING DEVELOPED THAT CAN TRANSMIT HIGH DEFINITION VIDEO.

38

I GOT A SONG STUCK IN MY HEAD TODAY.

That's why I'm standing here flipping the light switch on and off. I remember learning it at Bible camp, because we sang it at the beginning and end of each day. "From the rising of the sun to the going down of the same, the name of the Lord shall be praised." Have you ever heard it? I thought of it when I walked in and flipped on the lights a few minutes ago so

I could go to the bathroom. When I flipped them on, I thought "from the rising of the sun" and then kept humming the song the whole time I was on the pot. Then when I got to the door, I couldn't help singing "to the going down of the same" as I flipped the switch off.

I guess that's when I got stuck here at the switch, singing the first part and turning the light on and then singing the second as I turned off

 Q: WHAT DO YOU GET WHEN YOU CROSS A THOUGHT WITH A LIGHT BULB?
A: A BRIGHT IDEA!

the light. I'm going to quit in a minute, but I think I'm having one of those things people call a "God moment."

Those verses about God dividing the light from darkness kind of blow my mind about how awesome God is. In Genesis 1, verse 5 says: *"God called the light 'day,' and the darkness he called 'night.' And there was evening, and there was morning—the first day."*

THE FIRST DAY! Think about that! A beginning and an end. I'm so glad God didn't just decide to have us exist in day. God made sure that at the end of the day, there was night. Can you imagine how tired our eyes would be if we never got to the end of "day"?! It makes my eyes water just thinking about it.

So now, when I flip off the light as I'm leaving the bathroom, I hum that little song. I'm not as powerful as God is, but I can do good for the world. Don't forget to flush—and then use your power to flip that switch off too!

YOUR TURN

- **Have you ever had a "God moment" where you were just in awe of all God has done?**
- **How could flipping a light switch off be a way to show respect for God's creation?**
- **What worship songs get stuck in your head?**

 A COMPACT FLORESCENT LIGHT BULB USES 75 PERCENT LESS ENERGY THAN A REGULAR BULB AND IT CAN LAST UP TO FOUR YEARS.

39

HEAR MY EVIL LAUGH ...

Mmmwaaa, haaaaa, haaa, ha! Everyone is falling right into my evil plan. Or my *not-so-evil plan*, really.

I have been on a one-kid campaign to conserve energy by keeping our lights off in rooms we are not using. It's a little more fun if you plot and plan like you are some evil-doing villain. Now whenever Mom or Jasmin leave a room and forget to turn off the light, I make sure to give them a little reminder. Mom's harder to catch than Jasmin, but that's just because she has what she calls "years of practice." But she did leave the kitchen last night, and when I caught the light still on, I just started humming my song about the "rising of the sun, and the going down of the same." When she looked at me strangely, I gave a pointed look at the kitchen and said, "Oh, just remembering that God created light *and* darkness." I'm pretty sure I heard her mumbling something about having created a monster as she went back and switched off the light.

Q: WHAT IS A SUPERVILLAIN'S FAVORITE PART OF A JOKE?
A: THE *PUNCH* LINE!

Even with the sticky note Mom put up in here saying, "The light switch is God—Genesis 1:3-5," I could catch Jasmin any day, any time. She's as bad as I used to be, you know, way back before I learned my lesson two devotions ago. Just a little while ago, she left the bathroom light on, and I stood outside her door humming my song until she heard me and went back to flip the switch off. She doesn't even yell at me about why I'm humming anymore. But she does give me the stink-eye as she goes past. You'd think she'd appreciate what I'm trying to do here.

The other day I was reading in Paul's first letter to the Corinthians. In chapter 4 verse 2 he says, *"Now it is required that those who have been given a trust must prove faithful."* I kind of think that taking care of our world is like that—being faithful to take care of the things God provides. Speaking of taking care of things, be sure you flush when you're done.

If I can keep everyone remembering to turn off the light after they leave a room, why, we'll save up enough energy to take over the whole WORLD! Mmmwaaa, haa, haaa! Ha.

YOUR TURN

- **What kinds of things can you do that help you remember to take care of God's world?**
- **Walk through your home and look for ways you can take better care of all God has given you.**

 ONLY ONE-TENTH OF THE ENERGY A LIGHT BULB USES IS ACTUALLY TURNED INTO LIGHT. THE REST TURNS INTO HEAT INSTEAD.

40

DID YOU KNOW THAT people have different ideas of what clean looks like?

I know! I was a little baffled myself. I sorta understood it when Mom started saying things like my room "looks like the house caved in," and "I don't know how you sleep under all those books." I read books when I go to sleep, and not always the same one. Sometimes they pile up. Plus it never occurred to me that anyone cared how *my* room looks. Same goes in the bathroom. It turns out *Jasmin* thinks the bathroom is dirty all the time. (Mind blown.) When Mom brought it up, we went back and forth about what "clean" is, but it eventually came down to one word: poop. I'm just kidding. But that would be a funny life-lesson word. The word was *consideration*.

I KNOW A GOOD TOILET JOKE, BUT I'M NOT SUPPOSED TO USE POTTY TALK.

Being considerate means trying to make others happy more than yourself. Mom showed me a verse in Romans that made the point pretty well: Romans 14:14: *"I am convinced, being fully persuaded in the Lord Jesus, that nothing is unclean in itself."* (With you so far, Paul. Preach on.) *"But if anyone regards something as unclean, then for that person it is unclean."* What?

Mom did say she was "borrowing meaning" from a verse out of context, which just means the verse was originally about something else. Paul had friends who thought of certain foods as unclean. Basically, Paul is saying, "If you're doing something somebody is offended by, stop it." There are exceptions, but Mom insisted the meaning was the same in our bathroom: if Jasmin was put off by the toilet seat always being up and her books always getting knocked on the floor when I try to do handstands on the toilet, I should be more careful to tidy up in there. You should too. Oh, and don't forget to flush.

YOUR TURN

- **When have you realized that someone was bothered by something you did or left behind?**
- **What kinds of things bother you? Are you careful to be considerate to others about those things?**

 Q: WHAT DO YOU CALL IT WHEN YOU THROW THE LAST PAGE OF A COUPLE OF BOOKS IN THE TOILET? A: FLUSHING TWO CONCLUSIONS.

41

SOMETIMES I WISH
my little sister Jasmin
was a brother. Jim,
maybe. I don't know.
The name wouldn't
really matter. But if I
had a brother, then it
wouldn't be quite so
obvious who it is that
can't always hit the
mark when using the
toilet.

We may be going a little close to Too Much Information territory, but
I bet you know what I'm talking about. Even though I have definitely
learned the lesson of lifting the seat so no sprinkles offend, sometimes when I'm yawning or stretching or distracted, I miss. You know.
The target. Not by a mile. And I don't realize it from my perspective
right then, but when I come in later (if I look really hard for it) there's
a tiny, miniscule, almost imperceptible piddle puddle. Unless you are
Jasmin. Or Mom. And then, evidently it's all you can see.

When Jasmin made a big stink about it, I tried to convince Mom that
some of that particular mess was probably partly her mess also.

FUNNY TOILET SIGNS: FLUSH ME WELL AND KEEP ME CLEAN.
I'LL NEVER TELL WHAT I HAVE SEEN!

Mom didn't even respond. She just stared at me until I blinked and looked away.

"Yeah, you're right. It's my particular mess."

I went ahead and cleaned up my piddle puddle. It got me to thinking about Romans 14:14 again, so I went and looked at it afterward. Verse 13 says, *"Therefore let us stop passing judgment on one another."* I can get behind *that* part for sure. Then it continues, *"Instead, make up your mind not to put any stumbling block or obstacle in the way of a brother or sister."* So there it is again. It would be easier if my sister *was* a brother. He wouldn't mind. But I get that it doesn't mean "brother or sister" in that way. Mostly what it's saying is that my puddle is an obstacle for *others* that I have the power to prevent. Or at least clean up afterward. Consideration. It makes sense when you think about it. Oh yeah, don't forget to flush! That's considerate, too.

YOUR TURN

- Have you ever tried to ignore a bad habit in hopes that no one else notices?
- When something you do becomes an obstacle in your brother's or sister's or anyone else's way, how do you react when you become aware of it?
- Go ask someone close to you if they know of a bad habit you can try to get rid of.

 CLEAN A TOILET USING RUBBER GLOVES, DILUTED VINEGAR, A SCRUB BRUSH, AND PAPER TOWELS OR A WASH RAG.

42

AS I STOOD THERE, facing my nemesis, I cried out. "Why? Why? Why must you always conquer me?" I dropped to my knees and leaned back with my arms outstretched. "Why can I NOT remember to flush you?!"

I know. It's a little dramatic. But gee whiz. (Heh, heh. Whiz. Wizz.) Mom just sent me in here with a stern look and instructions to think about how inconsiderate it is to leave behind an unflushed bowl. Shaking my fist and glaring at the toilet with my lip curled up, I am frustrated at myself. It does seem like I'll never learn this lesson. But why? Why is it so hard for me? First I've got to remember to not knock any of my sister's stuff off onto the floor, and then I've got to remember to clean up my mess if I miss the target. And now? Now I've got to remember to flush even when missing the target isn't in question. You would think that it would be a lesson I've well and truly learned by now.

I went back and read some more of Romans 14. Verse 19 really stood out to me. It says, *"Let us therefore make every effort to do what leads*

 A ROYAL FLUSH IN THE GAME OF POKER INCLUDES THE ACE, KING, QUEEN, JACK, AND TEN ALL IN THE SAME SUIT.

to peace and to mutual edification." Edification is just a fancy word that means building somebody up. Do what leads to peace and building others up. I never thought I'd be thinking of a toilet as a way to make peace with my sister, but funnier things have happened.

I made myself a sticky note to keep as a reminder right by the toilet handle:

IF E = EVERY EFFORT
AND EVERY EFFORT = FLUSH + CLEAN
THEN ME + EE2 = PEACE.
THEREFORE, ME + CONSIDERATE TOILET PRACTICES = HAPPY MOM AND SISTER.

Hmm . . . I wonder if this is how Albert Einstein figured out some of the problems he solved? Whatever toilet math you come up with to be considerate, make sure you don't forget to flush!

YOUR TURN

- **Can you think of a lesson you have had to learn over and over in life?**
- **How can you give yourself reminders about consideration using Scripture?**
- **Walk through your home and bathroom looking for a way to show consideration to others.**

 IN NORTH AMERICA, THE FLUSHING HANDLE IS ALWAYS ON THE LEFT, DESPITE MOST PEOPLE BEING RIGHT HANDED.

43

DON'T MIND ME. I'm just going through the reading materials that we've gathered in here. *Everybody* keeps different stuff in the bathroom to read. Unless they don't read in the bathroom, which is totally WEIRD. And probably boring. What are ya gonna do, just go to the bathroom and leave?

Last week, my Sunday school teacher, Mrs. Johnson, started me thinking about what I read in here. She was teaching on Hebrews 5:11-12. The verses go like this: *"We have much to say about this, but it is hard to explain because you no longer try to understand. In fact, though by this time you ought to be teachers, you need someone to teach you the elementary truths of God's word all over again. You need milk, not solid food!"*

She put me on the spot because she knows Jasmin and I read a lot. She asked if my favorite book was the same as Jasmin's favorite book to read. "Of course not!" I said. Jasmin has just started chapter books and I like complicated adventure stories, sometimes even books in a

SIXTY-THREE PERCENT OF PEOPLE READ BOOKS, MAGAZINES, AND NEWSPAPERS WHILE IN THE BATHROOM.

series. Then Mrs. Johnson asked if my mom's favorite book was the same as my favorite book. "Of course not!" I said again. Mom's books have lots more words and lots less adventure. "But what if you had stopped growing in what you read and learned?" Mrs. Johnson asked. She pointed out that if I still relied on my old picture Bibles, I might not even hear these verses Paul spoke to the Hebrews.

When Paul said "You need milk, not solid food," he was saying people were stuck when they should have been going deeper in their faith. So I guess it's a good thing we have lots of different stuff in here to read. A couple of years ago I really enjoyed some of these same books that Jasmin reads. And sometimes they're a good easy reminder for me. But it would get really boring if I couldn't go deeper. Mrs. Johnson says it is "growing deeper" when you move on to more complex things.

I wonder what Mom keeps in her bathroom? Or Dad? I'm going to go check it out. Don't forget to flush when you're done with your own reading!

YOUR TURN

- **What are some simple truths about God that you go back to and remember often?**

- **Can you use those simple truths to figure out more complicated things about God?**

- **What is the most challenging thing you've learned when reading about God?**

89

"THE TOILETS AT A LOCAL POLICE STATION HAVE BEEN STOLEN. POLICE SAY THEY HAVE NOTHING TO GO ON." – RONNIE BARKER

44

I HATE IT WHEN I DON'T UNDERSTAND SOMETHING.

I'm good at reading. Really good. I read "above level," as my teachers like to say on parent night. Right before "struggles to pay attention sometimes." Anyway. So it kinda ticks me off when I run into words that I don't understand.

It's in my head because last weekend I was at Dad's apartment. Dad has always been a bit of a Bible nerd, always getting excited about some new thing he hadn't noticed in an ancient manuscript. I was in Dad's bathroom and found a book he was reading called *Christian Apologetics.* "Probably a good idea," I thought. "Who doesn't need to apologize sometimes?"

It wasn't about apologies. It was about really old, really smart people using big words to talk about things I couldn't understand about religion and God.

Dad pointed out that the book was "over my head a little" (a LITTLE?) and might make more sense down the road. He pointed me back to those verses in Hebrews 5. In verse 14 it says, *"But solid food is for the mature, who by constant use have trained themselves to distinguish good from evil."* Dad had a more *mature* knowledge about God and his faith. He'd earned it by always being willing to ask the next question and dig a little deeper. He admitted that even he didn't understand it all; he was just trying to learn more. It doesn't mean he's better than me. It just means he's spent more time thinking about God. And Kierkegaard, whoever that is. Maybe it's time that I move on from milk to meat in what I'm reading. I *do* read above my level, after all.

I've never thought about being picky about what I bring in here to read. Usually I just grab what I see on the way in or settle for what's already in here. If I plan ahead better, maybe I could move ahead from stories about faith to what faith actually means. Wooo. I got so deep there for a minute I almost forgot to flush! You'd better flush too.

YOUR TURN

- **How do you get smarter about things you don't learn in school? Like *what*, actually?**

- **Where did you learn most of what you know about God?**

- **What questions do you have about faith? (Ask someone who is more mature in their faith than you!)**

Q: KNOW WHAT THE NUMBER-ONE BATHROOM JOKE IS?
A: SORRY, I JUST FOUND OUT IT'S NUMBER TWO.

45

MOM THREATENED to either forbid reading in the bathroom or make me come up with a Dewey Decimal System for the stack of books and magazines next to the toilet. She has a point. I've realized that as good as I am

about bringing reading material *into* the bathroom, I do not excel at taking it *out.* The magazine table in our bathroom looks like a library that someone abandoned next to a toilet.

The stack is even bigger than usual, and it's my fault. I've been trying to figure out exactly where I am when it comes to my understanding of God. Well-intended grandmothers have given me Christian books since before I was born, and I still have them all. It all boils down to what level I want to achieve while I'm in here. Do I want to be amused? Cartoon Bible book. Do I want to be somewhat curious AND somewhat bored at the same time? Big doorstop grownup Bible. Do I want to be warmly engaged and possibly stretched a little? Harder to find. A devotional specifically targeting my age level and *designed* to be used in the bathroom? Now you're dreaming. Over the past few

THE BIBLE IS THE BEST-SELLING NONFICTION BOOK EVER.

days the stack has grown to a teetering point. I'm frustrated, because those verses from Hebrews 5 seem to suggest that milk is great when you're a kid but everybody needs to grow up and eat meat. I say I should be able to do both. Some of these books are like milk. Some are like burgers. I like both. What's wrong with that?

Mom says it's talking about knowing things about God—that while I'm young I know a little less than I will later on. She pointed out verse 12 from Hebrews 5: *"In fact, though by this time you ought to be teachers, you need someone to teach you the elementary truths of God's word all over again. You need milk, not solid food!"* She said the problem comes in when we're capable of learning bigger things and just decide not to learn them. I guess it would be like if Mrs. Johnson never read her Bible and still tried to tell us stories. It sure is helpful to have her help me understand the "meaty" parts of the Bible.

I can cut down my stack of books in here. I don't have to do all of my learning on the toilet, I guess. I bet if I ask someone at church, I can find some milk-level kids to give these picture books to. Hey, don't forget to flush!

YOUR TURN

- **Who helps you talk through stuff you don't understand right away when you read it or see it?**

- **When you open the Bible, do you feel like it's milk or steak? How can you get more familiar with it?**

 MCDONALDS SELLS 75 BURGERS EVERY *SECOND*, WHICH IS 6,480,000 A DAY. THIS GENERATES A LOT OF BATHROOM VISITS.

46

WHILE I WAS WORKING ON MY HOMEWORK THE OTHER DAY, all of a sudden I heard a thumping, pounding sound. I thought maybe Mom had put a quilt in the washer again and it was dancing around, bopping the walls before it exploded. Sometimes it does that. The dancing and bopping part. So far it hasn't exploded. But when I went to investigate

the problem, I heard that it was Jasmin banging on the wall to get someone's attention. She didn't care who. She was in a desperate spot. And since we're the only two who usually use our bathroom, I guess it was me who put her there. She was stuck with an empty roll.

"Eli! Mom! Somebody! I need your help. There's no toilet paper!" she yelled.

I hollered under the door, "It's okay Jas. I'm getting some." Darn. I remembered being in there just a while before her and using up

 THE FIRST RECORDED USE OF TOILET PAPER WAS IN SIXTH-CENTURY CHINA. PACKAGED TOILET PAPER WASN'T SOLD IN THE UNITED STATES UNTIL 1857.

the last of the roll. And usually I'm on it—what with the chart I keep and all. But I wanted to finish my homework fast so I could go outside to shoot some hoops, and I just forgot to do it.

After grabbing from Mom's bathroom and doing the hand-the-roll-through-the-door-with-your-head-turned thing, I went and looked up a verse that came to mind. It's from Proverbs 17:17 and says, *"A friend loves at all times, and a brother was born for adversity."* At first I thought it meant that a brother (like me) *causes* adversity. But it really means that someone close like a brother is there for you *in* times of difficulty or adversity. That's me! There in times of need. Except that I kind of also caused the time of need. Maybe if I could invent something that would pop a new roll out at you in case of an emergency. It could be my claim to fame. Then my forgetting to replace empties wouldn't be what Jasmin remembers.

While I work on that, don't you forget to flush!

YOUR TURN

- **Think of a time when you have put yourself before others. What could you have done differently?**

- **Do you know someone who is a good example of putting others first?**

- **Go and thank those who care for you. They often put you first when you don't even know it.**

 THE DAILY PRODUCTION OF TOILET PAPER IS ABOUT 83,048,116 ROLLS PER DAY.

47

AS AN APOLOGY,
I have constructed
a masterpiece of
toilet-paper art. This is
better than the spider
web I made—this
time I'm not wasting
anything, and you can
still move around the
bathroom without
ruining it. If you look
on either side of my
toilet-paper holder,
your eye will quickly
be drawn to the two
columns of TP that
begin at the floor on
either side of it. As the
columns rise above

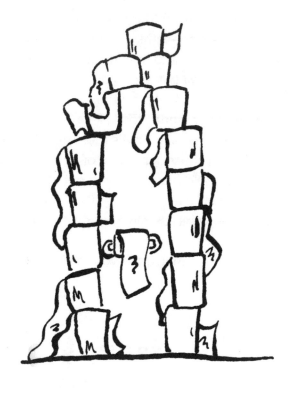

the toilet-paper holder, they join together to make one massive arch
that's just a little taller than I am.

I really did feel bad about leaving Jasmin without toilet paper, so I'm
taking consideration to the extreme. It *is* helpful that Mom sometimes

 70 PERCENT OF PEOPLE INSTALL TOILET PAPER SO IT UNROLLS TO THE OUTSIDE, OFF THE TOP.

shops in bulk. Jasmin could live in here for a year and probably not run out of toilet paper. To top it all off, I pulled off about a dozen squares to make a kind of banner above the toilet. I had to look it up, but I found a verse in 1 Corinthians 10:24 that works: *"No one should seek their own good, but the good of others."* I even wrote, "Sorry, Jas," at the bottom. Mom is going to be so proud. It all looks so sincere, and I even mean it.

Jasmin and I don't share everything. You may not even have a sibling to worry about. You may have it made in your own little toilet-paper paradise. But I bet you can find ways to show others you care—and not just here in the bathroom. I know Jasmin won't see this coming. I'm even going to try to find ways to be considerate to her *outside of the bathroom*. Crazy, right?

Alright. Don't forget to flush. I gotta get out of here—I don't want to ruin the surprise.

YOUR TURN

- **What's the best thing you've ever done to make up for forgetting to think about someone's feelings?**
- **How do you show other people you care about them?**

 30 PERCENT OF PEOPLE INSTALL TOILET PAPER THE *WRONG WAY*, SO IT ROLLS TO THE INSIDE, OFF THE BOTTOM.

48

WELL, BUMMER.

I was so certain that I was going to win "Person of the House" for this month. I *would* have to create the award in order to receive it, but I felt assured of victory. I'd solved Jasmin's toilet paper problems. What could be better?

Well, the trouble started when I opened the bathroom door to leave. Mom was standing there, nose nearly touching the door, with her hands on her hips. That's always a bad start. "I'm only asking to be polite instead of just accusing," she began, "but do you happen to know why there isn't *any* toilet paper in my bathroom, under my bathroom sink, or in the storage cabinet in the garage?"

Nuts.

 Q: WHY DOESN'T A PTERODACTYL MAKE ANY NOISE IN THE BATHROOM?
A: BECAUSE ITS "P" IS SILENT.

I may have gone overboard. I got so focused on Jasmin that I forgot mom also depended on our TP supply. Probably should have at least occurred to me when I took the roll off the holder in *her* bathroom. I tried to save it: "But Mom, I was thinking about Jasmin. See the banner about not seeking my good, but seeking hers?"

"I do," she replied. "Did you happen to read 1 Corinthians 10:23, the verse before it? It says, '*"I have the right to do anything," you say—but not everything is beneficial. 'I have the right to do anything'—but not all things are constructive.'* How about you reconstruct some of that toilet paper into my bathroom?"

It's not a real contest, but Mom could always one-up you in a Scripture contest. I forgot the first rule of being considerate to every-one around you: Be considerate to *everyone* around you. Everywhere. Oh, and don't forget to flush.

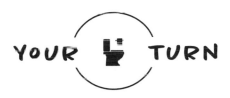

YOUR TURN

- **When have you had good intentions for being considerate go wrong? How did you recover?**

- **How can you make sure you're being *equally* considerate to everyone in your family?**

ON AVERAGE, THERE ARE 500 SQUARES OF TP ON A TWO-PLY ROLL. ALSO, ONE-PLY TP IS A CRIME AGAINST HUMANITY.

49

THERE WE STOOD.
Two pairs of socks,
ruined. This was *not*
how it was supposed to
have turned out. I knew
all about plungers from
before, but I realized
now there was more to
learn.

I was in my room when I
heard a wailing start up
in the bathroom and quickly reach an ambulance-siren decibel level.
I went running to save the day. When I reached the bathroom door,
where the giant noise was being created by my pipsqueak of a sister,
I knocked and she hollered for me to come and help. As I opened the
door to a quickly expanding puddle on the bathroom tiles, I kicked
my new shoes down the hall to safety and stepped in quickly. "Don't
worry, Jas. I've got this—I'm an expert!" I said with all the bravado of
a Navy hero able to stop the ship from sinking. I went for the plunger
and started giving it my best effort, but the overflow would not be
stopped. That's when the real hero saved the day. Mom leaned over
me with a quiet sneaker-clad step into the puddle and twisted the
little knob behind the toilet. After telling us to leave our socks in the
washer, she had us each use towels to help sop up the water.

DOUG MCMANAMAN SET A WORLD RECORD BY BALANCING A
BOWLING BALL ON A PLUNGER ON HIS CHIN FOR 49.39 SECONDS.

"Eli," she said, "I'm glad you were so quick to help, but maybe there's a more humble way of helping." While she left to talk to Jasmin, I did a quick search of Bible verses that have to do with humility. Proverbs 27:1-2 says, *"Do not boast about tomorrow, for you do not know what a day may bring. Let someone else praise you, and not your own mouth; an outsider, and not your own lips."*

Mom was pretty proud of me finding those verses when she came back to my room. She said so. I didn't even have to brag about it.

She said, "I was so proud at how fast you jumped in to help, and I'm even more pleased that you found these verses that can help remind you how to help in the future." After answering a few more questions about how to turn off the water flow at the knob, she left me feeling pretty good. And I realized it wasn't because I knew so much, but because she had said such good things about my trying so hard. "Let someone else praise you." Hmm. Very clever, Mom. Now—don't forget to flush!

YOUR TURN

- Is there something you feel like you're an expert at, and want others to know it?
- How do these verses change the way you might think or talk about that?
- Find someone doing something well and take time to share a word of praise. It feels good both ways.

 HUMILITY IS LIKE UNDERWEAR: ESSENTIAL, BUT INDECENT IF IT SHOWS.
— HELEN NIELSEN

50

I STOOD ONCE AGAIN IN FRONT OF THE TOILET, gripping the plunger like a baseball bat. I stared intently at its rubbery, apparently-not-a-hat part. I was determined not to go wrong again. Partly because Jasmin had not let up making fun of my failed rescue effort. Partly because I was running out of socks. But mostly because I don't like *failing*. I don't mind being humble. I just don't like being *humbled.*

I was poking around in Proverbs for a little while and bumped into another verse that reminded me of how I felt the other night—Proverbs 26:27. It says, *"Whoever digs a pit will fall into it; if someone rolls a stone, it will roll back on them."*

  JAZZ TRUMPETERS AND TROMBONISTS OFTEN USE THE HAT END OF A PLUNGER AS A MUTE FOR THEIR HORN.

I'm familiar with the scene. One day I'm in my yard digging a hole to China, and the next I've forgotten I dug the hole and trip into it playing soccer. The lesson is that there's almost always *one more thing* to think about. If you're pushing a big round rock up a hill, you can't just walk back down and think it won't come rolling after you. You can't hide your sister's unicorn pillow and think she's not going to deck you with it when she finds it. More to the point, the stuff I do doesn't just affect *me*. I got all big headed about my plunger skills and thought I was invincible. Instead of asking for help in the first place, I acted as though I could handle it alone.

The truth is, I *could* have handled it alone—if I'd remembered everything I'd learned about how to stop an overflowing toilet. But because I hurried, I didn't remember, and I actually made Jasmin's situation worse. Moral of the story? When it comes to helping others with your abilities, don't brag and don't rush. And don't forget to flush!

YOUR TURN

- **When have you been humbled by your own actions?**
- **When have you been able to turn that humility into something you could helpfully share with someone else?**

 WE DON'T KNOW WHO INVENTED THE PLUNGER, BUT WE'RE PRETTY SURE THEY NEEDED ONE.

51

I CAN SEE WHAT YOU'RE THINKING.

"Why, Eli," you're asking yourself, "do you have a laminated sign and painter's tape in the bathroom?" Well, I'll tell you.

I have realized that my best decisions aren't made in a panic. With that in mind, I've decided in a non-panicked state to remove the decision-making process from a situation where I regularly panic—by leaving myself instructions on a sign. The sign will actually benefit everyone at our house, which is something I've been trying to do lately. You should try it. Here's what it says:

1. DON'T PANIC.

(This I wrote in large, friendly letters. I also don't follow directions well in a panicked state, so I wanted to fix that at the beginning.)

104

 PLUNGERS HAVE BEEN USED TO GIVE CPR. TO PEOPLE. FOR REAL.

2. Turn off the water thingy.

3. Use the plunger. Try not to get water everywhere.

4. Turn water back on; test flush. Repeat steps 3 and 4 as needed.

I found something in Proverbs 4 that applies to lots of stuff, even outside of the bathroom. Proverbs 4:13 says, *"Hold on to instruction, do not let it go; guard it well, for it is your life."*

And without it, sometimes your life flashes before your eyes. That phrase, "for it is your life," really jumped out at me. A lot of times you forget you need instruction in your life until you *really, really* need the instruction. Like when I thought I was going to save the day for Jasmin and we ended up worse than when things started. So now I'm going to let the front of the toilet tank hold on to our instructions. And if there's nothing to panic about, maybe I won't forget to flush.

YOUR TURN

- **What other kinds of instructions have you learned about from the Bible?**
- **Who teaches or instructs you in your faith?**
- **What is something you've learned recently about faith?**

 There are separate designs for sink plungers and toilet plungers.

52

"A MIGHTY FORTRESS IS OUR GOD . . . A SOMETHING SOMETHING SUH UH UM THINGGGGG." Ow, I got shampoo in my eye. I can't get this song out of my head, and I can't remember the second line. We sang it at church Sunday and somehow I can't forget it or remember it all at the same time—so here I am in the shower belting out the six words I know. "A MIIIIGHTY . . ." Shoot, how does that *end*? I'm allowed to get loud in the shower, but sometimes I can get *too* loud. Here, watch: "A MIIIIGHTY FOOR TRESS IIIIIIIS OUR GOOOOOD . . ."

[thumping on the door] "ELI! Knock it off!"

"But Mom, I'm *praising*."

"God says to praise later when you know more of the words."

"But what's *next*?"

"It's about a bulwark. GET OUT. We can look it up together."

 MOST PEOPLE HAVE A VOCAL SINGING RANGE OF TWO OCTAVES.

Mom's snappy comeback game is strong. I do like praising God by singing, especially in the shower. Mom must have felt a little bad about shooting me down for praising—I just found a note in my shoe with some verses from Psalm 150 in it, starting with verse 1:

"Praise the LORD. Praise God in his sanctuary; praise him in his mighty heavens. Praise God in a way that doesn't disturb the neighbors, and try to remember that the bathroom isn't soundproof. Praise the Lord!"

Wait a minute . . . I think she's messing with me again. Yup, I looked it up. Everything after *mighty heavens* was Mom being a smarty-pants. I'll admit that I get a little carried away and "unaware of my surroundings," as mom likes to say. If you promise not to tell anyone, I might even admit I sometimes do it on purpose. I think Mom is trying to remind me that I can praise God and not annoy people at the same time. Oh, look. On the back she's all sweet-mommy again: "I cried a little about how happy it makes me that you sing hymns in the shower. I love you, baby."

Gross. At least I don't have to feel bad about singing anymore. Score! Oh right—somebody would probably love it if you don't forget to flush.

YOUR TURN

- **When do you get to make loud, awesome noise to God? What's your favorite way or time to praise?**
- **People enjoy different kinds of praising God. Ask some of the grownups in your life about their favorites.**

 THE HYMN "A MIGHTY FORTRESS IS OUR GOD" WAS WRITTEN BY MARTIN LUTHER AND BASED ON PSALM 46.

53

FOR LIKE A MILLION YEARS we've been out of dog shampoo. That has been A-OK with me. I haven't had to give Muttley a bath in forever. Until today. Mom finally remembered to put dog shampoo on the list and brought some home so I could take care of Muttley, who according to mom, "stinks to high heaven." When I started to suggest maybe his smell was a pleasing offering, she shut me down before I could even form the complete sentence. Pointing at me and Muttley, she said, "You. That. Dog. Now." When Mom starts putting periods between words, I get busy real quick, 'cause she's not kidding around.

So here I am, covered half in bubbles, half in fur, and all over in wet dog dirt. But here comes the fun part. When I use my super high singing voice, Muttley joins me in singing praises! "A MIIIIGHTY FOOORTRESS IIIIIIIS OUR GOOOOO . . ."

A DOG CAN LEARN TO UNDERSTAND UP TO 200 WORDS!

"Aaaarrrooooooowoooooowoooo!" sang Muttley.

Aaaahhhahaha! Oh my gosh, that cracks me up. Mom's vacuuming, and Jasmin's got her radio going, so we could do this all day.

That Psalm 150 that Mom "modified" the other day? It ends in verse six, saying *"Let everything that has breath praise the Lord. Praise the Lord."* And oh, wow, does Muttley have *breath*! If Muttley praised his breath into Mom's face, I'd have to brush his teeth in addition to the bath. "A MIIIGHTY . . ."

"Aaaarrrooowoooowooo!" Glorious praise music! This is so much fun. Don't get so distracted you forget to flush!

YOUR TURN

- **What do you think "let everything that has breath praise the Lord" means?**
- **Can you imagine animals everywhere praising God? Maybe it's not so different than what we hear when we listen to the world around us.**
- **Take a deep breath. While you breathe it out, think of all the things you can praise God for.**

54

I HAVE BEEN TRYING TO IMAGINE A FULL ORCHESTRA IN MY BATHTUB SHOWER.

After singing praises with Muttley yesterday, I went back and looked at Psalm 150 again. There's a lot going on in that short little psalm. Verses 3, 4, and 5 say, *"Praise him with the sounding of the trumpet, praise him with the harp and lyre, praise him with timbrel and dancing, praise him with the strings and pipe, praise him with the clash of cymbals, praise him with resounding cymbals."*

That is all kinds of praising in all kinds of ways! Since singing in the shower is one of my favorite ways to sing praises, I started trying to do the math on fitting all those things into my tub. If I'm holding a trumpet with one hand and strumming a harp with the other, I could tap my foot on a tambourine. But that's going to make it harder to do the dancing mentioned. I'll have to be very careful there. I really like

A MAN NAMED SAM ONCE PLAYED A TOTAL OF FIVE INSTRUMENTS—POCKET TRUMPET, HARMONICA, ELECTRIC BASS, ELECTRIC GUITAR, AND PIANO—AT THE SAME TIME FOR A WORLD RECORD.

the idea of cymbals in the shower. But somehow I missed the flute and lyre. Whatever a lyre is.

Of course, the psalm doesn't say anything about all this taking place in the shower. But wouldn't that be something?! Maybe there's a Guinness record for most instruments played in the shower. Music always sounds better there. Something about the good acoustics. And if you want to praise God, you want to make it sound good, right?

I'm not sure if Mom is all in on this idea. When I asked her at breakfast today if there was such a thing as a waterproof trumpet, she got very quiet and suspicious looking. Jasmin just rolled her eyes. While you think on it, don't forget to flush.

YOUR TURN

- **What other ways are there besides music to praise God?**
- **When you think of praising God in song, do you have a favorite song?**
- **Find out what someone else's favorite praise song is.**

Q: WHAT IS A DOG'S FAVORITE INSTRUMENT?
A: A TROMBONE.

55

GROSS! AWW, MAN . . .

I got something on my favorite shirt. I can't see it, because it's on the end of my elbow, but I can FEEL it. And I can see what's left of a grimy smudge on the counter. Sadly, I did not see *that* a moment ago before sticking my elbow in it.

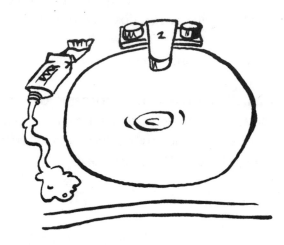

You might think that with me being a boy, I would be the messy one in the family. You might be right, but be careful making assumptions. However. I do *not* leave globs of toothpaste on the sink counter in the bathroom. Yuck! How could you just walk away after setting someone up for a mess like that? My sister does it ALL THE TIME! I've filed a complaint about it. With both parental units: Mom here, and Dad when we stay at his place. Evidently, though, that's not going to get me any help. Last time I brought it up with Mom, she said, "It might be easier to have the whole world to yourself, but it sure would be boring."

KNOCK, KNOCK! WHO'S THERE? ALICE! ALICE WHO?
ALICE FORGIVEN!

I'm pretty sure I'd be okay with boring sometimes. But since I know she wants me to "grow in character" (she *loves* that phrase), I went and looked up some verses that are made for just this kind of situation. Colossians 3:13 says, *"Bear with each other and forgive one another if any of you has a grievance against someone. Forgive as the Lord forgave you."* When I saw it written like that, I realized how small of a problem one gloppy elbow is compared to how often the Lord forgives me. I actually wrote it out on a sticky note and put it up on our bathroom mirror. It helps me keep in check the frustration that often comes with sharing a bathroom. I read that note and then imagine Jasmin giving thanks in her heart for having such a tidy brother to share the bathroom with. Then I giggle just a little.

Hey—don't forget to flush! It won't hurt anything for you to go wipe down your sink after that. You know—just in case.

YOUR TURN

- **Sometimes living with people can be frustrating. Think of some of the things others do that frustrate you.**
- **How do you "forgive as the Lord forgave"?**
- **Now think of some of the things you do that might frustrate others. How can you adapt so others might benefit?**

113

Q: WHAT HELPS YOU KEEP YOUR TEETH TOGETHER?
A: TOOTHPASTE.

56

DARN IT.

I did everything right.
I got annoyed about
Jasmin's toothpaste
globs yesterday, but
before I got out of the
bathroom I got over
it and *I even used the
Bible* to help me get
over it. It was perfect.
Then later I got mad
about something else
Jasmin did and I made
some smart-alec

comment about her ruining the elbow of my favorite shirt with her
toothpaste.

Stupid clothing. Clothing. Clothe yourself . . . what am I remembering?

Oh wait, I think it was in Colossians. Yep, right next to the other verse
I used to calm myself down about this in the first place. Colossians 3,
verse 12: *"Therefore, as God's chosen people, holy and dearly beloved,
clothe yourselves with compassion, kindness, humility, gentleness and*

HERE'S SOMETHING TO LIE AWAKE THINKING ABOUT: WHY ISN'T IT
CALLED *TEETHPASTE?*

patience." I bet it's a lot harder to get toothpaste on compassion and kindness. Now I'm giggling a little about putting together a niceness outfit. "Mom, does this gentleness match this patience?"

Darn it, Mom overheard me. "You're such a goofball, Eli. But it's good to hear you're ready to make peace with Jas again. I was just coming by to point out that toothpaste is actually a cleaning agent."

Mom thinks of *everything*. Now I'm back here, washing my elbow. Well, the elbow of my shirt. A little warm water, and my world should return to order. I do want to be good and nice to my sister. And I do love her. But when my elbow is minty fresh (and plaque free, apparently) sometimes it's easier to poke at her than forgive her. I'm trying to get better, honest. Are you better about remembering to flush yet?

YOUR TURN

- **Who in your family knows the quickest way to upset you?**
- **How can you be even quicker at forgiving them?**
- **How can *you* avoid upsetting the people you live with—especially upsetting them on purpose?**

 Q: WHY WAS THE TOOTHPASTE CRYING ALL THE TIME?
A: IT WAS THE SENSITIVE TYPE OF TOOTHPASTE.

57

I MAY HAVE OVER-STATED THINGS when I said Jasmin is the one who always messes things up in the bathroom. On the weekend after the now-famous elbow incident, we went to stay at Dad's place. Saturday morning I was up first. I was in a good, do-everything-I'm-supposed-to-do mood, so I brushed my teeth, ate some breakfast, and even brushed my teeth again just for grins before plopping down on the couch for some serious early-morning video-game time. About an hour and a half later, I heard Dad come out of his bedroom. He shuffled past to the kitchen, pausing to wave and mumble, "Hey." He made coffee, then joined me. "Eli," he said, "can I ask you something? When you rinse your mouth after brushing your teeth, are you just spitting it out right at the mirror?"

What?

 IN SONG OF SOLOMON 6:6, SOLOMON SAYS HIS GIRLFRIEND'S TEETH LOOK LIKE SHEEP. WHAT A COMPLIMENT!

He led me back to the bathroom and pointed to the mirror. Indeed, it looked like a toothbrush had been murdered on it. "I don't . . ." I began and then trailed off.

"I've seen you do it, especially when you're tired," he said gently. "You're not spitting, you're just letting your mouth hang open while you brush. The bristles are flicking toothpaste off your teeth and all over the mirror." Omigosh he's right. I totally do that. It's Jasmin's chore to clean my toothpaste mess off the mirror at home, and she never says anything about it. She didn't even mention it during all the grief I gave her about getting her glob on my elbow. Wow. Who'd have guessed you could learn so much about yourself from toothpaste?

I'm starting to recognize how much I'm forgiven and loved in life without even realizing it. That's what the third verse in that passage from Colossians 3 talks about. Verse 14 says love is the most important: *"And over all these virtues put on love, which binds them all together in perfect unity."*

I don't know about perfect unity, but I sure know I'm loved. Show somebody you love them and don't forget to flush!

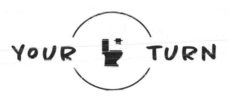

YOUR TURN

- **Where do you feel most loved in life?**
- **Where do you have opportunities to show love to family?**

 Q: WHAT TIME SHOULD YOU ALWAYS GO TO THE DENTIST?
A: RIGHT AFTER TOOTH-HURTY.

58

I HAD SUCH A GREAT SYSTEM WORKING, AND JESUS HAD TO GO AND RUIN IT.

You know how when you get out of the shower there's no good way to find out if the towel is already wet? Sure, you could check it before you get *in* the shower, but who plans ahead like that? I had a foolproof method: after you use a towel once, ball it up and leave it in the floor. That way you know if it's balled up, it's probably still wet.

Mom shut me down on that one, and quick. I was barely a couple of days into my plan when Mom said something about how we "don't have paid servants around here, kid" and something about Jasmin being tired of stepping out of the shower onto wet, balled-up towels. Somewhere between *towels* and *servants* and mentioning Jasmin's feet, something clicked. Suddenly I was transported to the middle of the grossest sermon I've ever heard.

Q: WHAT GETS WETTER THE MORE IT DRIES?
A: A TOWEL.

It was from John 13:1-9. Why gross? The preacher went into a lot of detail about how filthy everyone's feet got in Jesus' time. I remember her saying something about "dust *caking*" on their feet and "granules of sand" getting jammed up between their toes. Yuck. At important gatherings, it was a servant's job to clean all of those nasty feet. But check out what Jesus did in verse 5: *"After that, he poured water into a basin and began to wash his disciples' feet, drying them with the towel that was around him." Jesus* did a servant's job! For the people around him! He was willing . . . "ELI." I snapped out of my reverie. Mom was standing in the bathroom looking at me. "So what are you going to do with that balled-up towel, Eli?"

"If it bothers Jas, I'll stop leaving towels on the floor. It's what Jesus would do." I put the towel in the hamper and walked out past Mom, who seemed almost concerned that I'd figured out the right thing to do. You know the right thing to do—don't forget to flush!

YOUR TURN

- **Where can you offer courtesy to the people in your home?**
- **In what new ways could you show care that would be unexpected awesomeness for them?**

 PITTSBURGH STEELERS FOOTBALL FANS LIKE TO WAVE A THING THEY CALL THE "TERRIBLE TOWEL." MAYBE IT JUST NEEDS TO BE WASHED.

59

DON'T MIND ME.
I'm just hanging up
some fresh towels.
Mom is still keeping a
close eye on me, and
I overheard her whis-
pering to Dad on the
phone that she wasn't
sure what was going on.
Sometimes I *do* get it.
And when I do, I really
get a kick out of blow-
ing everyone's mind
with how *well* I get it.

One of the funny things from the verses in John 13 about Jesus
washing the disciples' feet is in verse 6. Just like I'm standing here
holding a towel, Jesus stood holding his towel. *"He came to Simon
Peter, who said to him, 'Lord, are you going to wash my feet?'"* I'd like to
read at least one translation that followed that up with Jesus saying,
"Well, duh!" Sometimes those guys were a little slow to catch on. A
lot of the times when they are, it makes me feel better about having
to learn and re-learn this God stuff all the time.

 COMMON GUIDELINES RECOMMEND WASHING BATH TOWELS EVERY
THREE TO FOUR USES.

Kind of like a few minutes ago. I was hanging up the first fresh towel on the rod. Right then, Jasmin walks by. She stops and says, "Are you putting up clean towels?" Fortunately I didn't say, "Well, duh," just like Jesus didn't say that. I'm pretty sure that would have kind of ruined the whole *service* vibe I was going for. So I just said, "Sure. I know how much you hate finding wet towels around, so I've decided to make sure there are dry ones ready for showers."

My sister does not know how to handle me when I talk to her like that. So instead of just walking on or saying something nice back, she acted like I'd zapped her and proceeded to clutch her chest and slide gasping down the doorframe until she collapsed into a giggling heap in the floor. Although after she walked away, I'm almost certain I heard her say, "Thanks." Of course, she may have been talking to God.

Why not thank God for someone serving you from time to time? Then serve others by not forgetting to flush.

YOUR TURN

- **Why is it sometimes hard for people who *live together* to serve one another?**
- **What kinds of things can you do to make serving others in your home easier?**
- **Think of one act of service that will blow the minds of those who live with you. Go and do it!**

 JOHN EVANS SET THE RECORD FOR BALANCING A CAR ON HIS HEAD FOR 33 SECONDS. THE ONLY PADDING HE USED? A FOLDED-UP TOWEL!

60

I HAVE TO ADMIT THAT I KIND OF GOT A BIG HEAD ABOUT THE WHOLE TOWEL/SERVICE THING. When I saw Mom and Jasmin's minds get blown by it, I did it at Dad's place too. I had everyone looking at me strangely as I hummed and went about routinely making sure everyone had a clean, dry towel to use. For a minute, I started to think maybe I was doing a better job of this whole service thing than anyone else.

It was Dad who stepped in to talk with me as I was straightening the towels I had just situated on their hooks by the shower at his place. "Whatcha up to, Eli?" Well, you don't have to ask me twice to toot my own horn. I told Dad about Jesus washing his disciples' feet and explained how I was showing courtesy by serving others. My eyebrows rose a little as I said, "Just like Jesus!" I'm pretty sure that's when Dad knew I was a little self-inflated. He played it cool though, and fortunately didn't just take a needle to my ego.

 IMPORTANT MEN USED TO HAVE TRUMPET PLAYING HERALDS TO ANNOUNCE THEIR GREATNESS. IF SOMEONE CAUSES THEIR OWN LOUD FANFARE, THEY ARE TOOTING OR BLOWING THEIR OWN HORN.

He said, "Let's go look at that again, son. I'm curious to see how the rest of that foot-washing, towel-wielding story goes." So we found it and read it again. This time, Dad made sure I kept reading through what Jesus said after washing the disciples' feet—all the way to verse 16, which read, *"I tell you the truth, no servant is greater than his master, nor is a messenger greater than the one who sent him."* When Dad suggested I re-read that verse, I started to understand what he was doing. As I looked at it again, I realized that I had started to pat myself on the back so hard I wasn't thinking straight. Jesus had not washed his disciples' feet because he wanted to be *right* or to blow anyone's mind. He did it as a way to show humility and love.

I think I'm going to keep trying to keep the towels in order, but I'll work on not letting myself feel too puffed up about it. You, though, should definitely remember to flush.

- How does it feel when you do something nice for someone and they don't thank you?
- How do you think your focus could change to handle it more like Jesus?
- Watch for someone showing courtesy who might ordinarily be overlooked.

 KNOCK, KNOCK! WHO'S THERE? THE TRUTH. NO JOKE.

JAS AND I GET READY FOR SCHOOL AT THE SAME TIME,

which means some shared bathroom time most mornings. I'll be honest: neither of us loves this time. We're just not morning people. One time Mom had to draw a line down the middle of the mirror on the back of the door so we could each have a side to comb our hair without shoving. We mostly stopped.

"Why are you parting your hair from left to right, Eli?" Jas's question puzzled me. "I'm not. It's picture day, so I thought I'd do something new. And I'm parting it from right to left." "It's left to right," she replied. "JAS," I said, getting annoyed. It's my head. I know where I'm parting it. On the RIGHT, to the left. What are you talking about?" I turned to look at her. With her finger, she traced a line on my forehead. "*Left* to *right*," she said, getting it completely backwards.

Suddenly I got it. From her perspective, it went from left to right, even though on my actual head it went from the right side to the left side. At least from *my* perspective, which is the one I usually roll with. Naturally, this bothered me all day. I was distracted in class.

IF YOU WRITE FROM RIGHT TO LEFT WITH THE LETTERS FLIPPED BACKWARD, YOU CAN READ IT FORWARD IN THE MIRROR.

Contemplative on the bus. "WHICH WAY DID I PART MY HAIR?" my brain screamed at itself.

Mom found me in the bathroom later that night at the mirror, where I'd been standing for half an hour trying to figure out which way my hair was going. I explained my quandary. "I read a verse this morning that might help; it's Proverbs 18:2," she said. "It goes, *'Fools find no pleasure in understanding, but delight in airing their own opinions.'*"

"Thanks for taking time out of your day to call me a fool, Mom. 'Preciate ya." I frowned.

"That's not what I'm saying. If we're only interested in airing our opinions, we're not showing humility. When you were standing in here this morning arguing about which way your hair went, *that* was a little foolish. But you spent the whole day trying to understand your sister's perspective. *That* makes you a good brother."

Oh, Mom. So right so often. Don't be foolish—don't forget to flush!

YOUR TURN

- Are you more likely to dig in and defend your own opinion, or do you listen to others well?
- What kind of attitude might make others more willing to hear your perspective?
- Why is it important to learn from others' perspectives?

 IF EYES ARE THE WINDOW TO YOUR SOUL, ARE MIRRORS THE WINDOW TO YOUR FACE?

62

WHEN I WALKED IN HERE A LITTLE WHILE AGO, I stood looking at myself in the mirror because I forgot what I had come in for. It's okay. Happens all the time. It usually comes to me. But then I noticed a cute little Jasmin handprint on the mirror. While I tried to remember why I was in here, I put my hand over her handprint

to see the difference in size. My hand was like some kind of big Yeti hand over hers. Or do Yetis have paws? Good thing I'm not a Yeti. Although it might be kinda cool . . .

Sorry. My mind is still wandering. And Jasmin has been driving me nuts. There was the thing about which way I was parting my hair. And all day today she's been tagging along after me and wanting me to play games that are just silly. I lost my patience, and now I'm feeling bad because I hollered at her to leave me alone. Now looking at the image of my gigantic Yeti hand covering her smaller handprint, I started realizing how different her perspective is from mine. For

THE LEGEND OF THE YETI COMES FROM NEPAL, WHICH TELLS OF AN APE-LIKE CREATURE THAT IS TALLER THAN THE AVERAGE HUMAN.

some reason, a Bible verse that I memorized two summers ago popped into my head. First Corinthians 13:11 says, *"When I was a child, I talked like a child, I thought like a child, I reasoned like a child. When I became a man, I put the ways of childhood behind me."* Here's where Dad would say, "Whoa there, Eli. Slow up. You're not a man yet." I agree. I have no desire to give up afternoon snacks, video games, and having someone drive me everywhere. But it does make me consider how I should react to her as my younger sister. I'm older, but Mom and Dad never made me feel bad for being a little kid. And she's only a couple of years younger, anyway.

If I squat down a few inches, I can look at myself in the mirror from her height. I don't remember being that much shorter than I am now, but seeing so much ceiling when looking in the mirror seems like a familiar memory. When I stand up again to my height, there's much more floor than ceiling in the reflection. And the toilet. OH, RIGHT! That's what I came in here for. I forgot to flush. Don't you forget!

YOUR TURN

- **How do you think your perspective is different than those you live with?**

- **What do you think it means when the Bible says "thought like a child" and "reasoned like a child"?**

- **Think of one way your thinking has changed as you've grown up.**

 Q: **WHAT DID THE YETI SAY TO THE ABOMINABLE SNOWMAN?**
A: **YOU'RE UNBELIEVABLE!**

63

WHEN I WONDER ABOUT SOMETHING, I usually go and look it up. I started thinking about that verse about putting away childish ways and went to read it in my Bible so I could see what was before and after it. I'd rather find things out on my own that way than be told to go look it up. And if I'm not fast, Mom is pretty

quick to put the suggestion out there. When *I* look it up, it was because *I* wanted to. Totally different from doing it for someone else.

If you read all of 1 Corinthians 13, you'll see that all the verses before 11 are about *love this* and *love that*. But the verse after it is kind of interesting. Verse 12 says, *"For now we see only a reflection as in a mirror; then we shall see face to face. Now I know in part; then I shall know fully, even as I am fully known."* Obviously, it became experiment time.

I got Jasmin to come in the bathroom with me so she could look at my actual face and then the reflection of my face. Because, duh, I can't look at my own face without a mirror. It might have looked funny

 I THINK I WANT A JOB CLEANING MIRRORS. IT'S JUST SOMETHING I CAN SEE MYSELF DOING. BUT ON REFLECTION, IT COULD BE A PANE.

to anyone walking by, me with the side of my face pressed up against the mirror and Jasmin standing directly in front of me with her eyes darting back and forth between "face" and "mirror face."

After several minutes I asked her if she could tell anything different between me and my reflection. She said, "I can see every bump and freckle on your face, and I can see every bump and freckle on your reflection. But . . ." She dramatically paused. "I can't do this to your reflection!" and then she honked my nose and scrambled out to the safety of her room.

Other than the nuisance of having to blow my nose because she honked it, I still found myself staring at my reflection. Mom, Dad, Mrs. Johnson, my pastor—they've all said we reflect God's love. But this verse says that to fully know love, we will see that love face to face. That's a pretty cool thought.

Don't forget to flush while you think on that.

YOUR TURN

- **Who in your life do you know in a fully face-to-face way? Can you imagine knowing God like that?**
- **Why does a Bible chapter about love focus on growing and knowing?**
- **Go and look really closely at someone you care for. Tell them how much you love them.**

129

 Q: WHY CAN'T YOUR NOSE BE 12 INCHES LONG?
A: BECAUSE THEN IT WOULD BE A FOOT!

64

I HAVE TO FESS UP.
I have been plotting.
Sometimes it feels
like God just *knows*.
It's kind of like the way
mom always seems
to know—only more
intense, and sometimes
a little more amazing.

It kind of stuck in my
head back when that basketball coach told me I wasn't big enough
for the team yet. I started formulating a plan that had to happen while
I was staying with Dad, on account of the really old scale he has in his
bathroom. It's avocado green and gives a very different weight than I
get on the one here at Mom's. AND it has a little knob on the side that
you can turn to move the needle above or below zero. I'm pretty sure
he doesn't realize that and I need him to say I'm big enough to try out
for wrestling.

So just as my mind began to imagine what the right weight to accom-
plish my goal might be, I decided to see how much I weigh while
holding my Bible. Not much more than without it, it turns out. What
was really crazy, though, is that I opened up my Bible randomly and
God spoke to me. Not like "booming voice" speaking. But the words

 **AN EPHAH IS A HEBREW UNIT OF DRY MEASURE EQUAL TO
APPROXIMATELY ONE BUSHEL, OR ABOUT 33 LITERS.**

at the top corner of the page seemed like they were written just for me in that moment. Leviticus 19:35-36 was right there staring at me. I even imagined seeing my name before the first word. *"(Eli) Do not use dishonest standards when measuring length, weight or quantity. Use honest scales and honest weights, an honest ephah and an honest hin. I am the Lord your God, who brought you out of Egypt."*

I'm not sure what an ephah or a hin might be, but I'm pretty sure they won't undo what the first part of those verses are saying to me. Part of me wants to be all "Sheesh, why do you have to go and ruin my plans, God?" But the other part of me feels a little tingly after feeling like God's word spoke directly to what I was thinking about. That part realizes how silly it would be to argue with God. Flipping open the Bible isn't a magic trick for hearing from God, but I guess I'm glad I bumped into that verse.

Don't forget to flush!

YOUR TURN

- Why do you think God cares about people using honest scales and weights?
- Is there a struggle you face that God would want you to deal with fairly?
- How different would you feel if God spoke those words out loud to you?

 A HIN IS A HEBREW UNIT OF LIQUID CAPACITY EQUAL TO APPROXIMATELY 5.5 QUARTS OR 5 LITERS.

65

BUMMER. DAD GOT A NEW SCALE.

Good thing I had decided that I wasn't going to cheat and make the scale say I weigh more than I do. I arrived at Dad's to find that cheating was off the table anyway . . . or floor, I guess. In place of the avocado museum

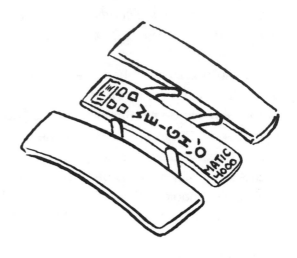

piece of a scale I was expecting, I came in to find a shiny, modern digital scale. Dad got so into telling me about it that it didn't cross his mind right away why I even asked about it. Turns out the new scale can track the weight of four different people and even communicate that information to Dad's phone.

I don't know why he'd want that, but I'm glad he's happy with his purchase. On 364 days of the year, I don't care what I weigh. But on the day I'm trying out for some sport, I really don't want to hear another coach tell me I'm not big enough to play. No biggie—those verses from Leviticus aren't letting me off the hook. Leviticus 19:35 gets right

THE EARLIEST DESIGN FOR A SPRING SCALE MEASURING WEIGHT DATES TO 1770 CE FOR A SCALE MADE BY RICHARD SALTER.

to the point: *"Do not use dishonest standards when measuring length, weight, or quantity."*

No real surprise here: the Bible seems to be against dishonesty. Alert the press! I guess it means not just about *actual* weight and ways of measuring things—like when you stand up on your tippy-toes at the amusement park trying to be taller than the captain's sword. It's talking about not shading the truth in your favor anywhere in your life. Like when the coffee table got scratched while me and Jas were wrestling in the living room, but I managed to make it sound like I hadn't even been at home when Mom asked about it later. I tried shading the details in my favor, but the truth eventually seems to come out.

It's just better to keep things honest in the first place. And flushed— don't forget to flush.

YOUR TURN

- **When was the last time you told a story with the details shaded to put you in a good light?**
- **How can you stay aware of how honest you're being?**

 IN BIBLE TIMES, LENGTH WAS MEASURED WITH THE FOREARM, HAND, OR FINGER.

66

SO NOW I KNOW THAT (WITHOUT MY BIBLE)

I weigh 75.2 pounds on mom's scale, and, according to Dad's phone, 77.205 pounds or 34.112 kilograms on his scale. (Thanks, Dad, for texting me my weight.) It really wasn't hard for me to adjust to the idea of just being honest with coach about what I weigh. The third verse from that section of Leviticus 19 helped—verse 37:

"Keep all my decrees and all my laws and follow them. I am the LORD."

It's the kind of sentence that grabs your attention; it's like the whole room would get quiet if you read it out loud. Actually, it sounds like the kind of thing mom says right before she closes the door at lights out when I have a sleepover. "Keep all my decrees. I am the MOM. If I see any of you before dawn, no pancakes."

THE EARLIEST DOCUMENTED WRESTLING MATCH TOOK PLACE IN THE EIGHTH CENTURY B.C. AT THE ANCIENT OLYMPIC GAMES.

Mom doesn't really have to do that. It's not like our house rules about bedtime changed. She's just reminding us who is in charge. That's how verse 37 sounds to me, like God's just reminding everyone that God sets the standard, and that we're supposed to be honest about how well we're following it. There's no point in pretending that we're following God any better than we are. God is like the scale—you can tell God whatever you want, but God knows the truth. So I'm not mad at the scales. I weigh what I weigh. The scales will keep track for me. Dad's will probably send me emails with my BMI stats after each visit.

The good news about God? God loves us no matter what. The good news about what I weigh? Turns out that in wrestling they have *different weight classes*. I'm exactly the right size to wrestle kids my size, so I'm trying out for that this year.

You're exactly the right size to flush that toilet—so don't forget.

YOUR TURN

- **What are some of your family's "ground rules," the ones that are rarely spoken but always obeyed?**
- **How do those rules help your family live together?**

COMPETING WRESTLERS ARE DETERMINED SOLELY ON THEIR AGE AND BODY WEIGHT, AS OPPOSED TO BELT RANK OR SKILL LEVEL.

WORLD

67

THIS ONE TIME DAD TOOK US TO THE AQUARIUM IN TOWN. We especially love the otters, because . . . because *otters*, dude. Otters are awesome. Before we left the aquarium that day, we all went to the bathroom. Dad and I went to the one for boys and Jasmin went to the one for girls. Obviously. We were done first so we went and stood near—but not *creepy* near—the ladies' room door, and waited.

And waited. Aaaaannnnd waited. She seemed to be taking forever. I started comparing the outlines on the signs for men's and ladies' room doors, and wondering why whoever made them thinks that all ladies wear dresses all the time. At first I thought Dad looked a little restless, but I eventually realized he was getting worried.

"What are you worried about, Dad?" I asked. "Jasmin is on the other side of that door," he said, "and there's not a lot I can do to see if she's okay. I'm sure she's fine; I just get nervous sometimes." "Ask, and the door shall be opened to you," I replied. "It's in the Bible."

A DUTCH DOOR IS SEPARATED IN HORIZONTAL HALVES, WHILE A FRENCH DOOR SPLITS VERTICALLY.

"What?" Dad's head turned. I suddenly had his full attention. "Ask, and it shall be opened," I answered. "Mom told us about it." I thought he knew that one.

"Your mom is a smart lady," Dad said, "and I bet she told you *knock* and it will be opened, because that's what Luke 11:9 says: *'Ask, and it will be given to you; seek and you will find; knock and the door will be opened to you.'* It's about reaching out in faith, and it's not a bad idea. That door is an obstacle between us and Jasmin right now, but there's nothing separating us from God. What say we pray for Jasmin for a minute?" Sounded good to me. We bowed our heads and Dad prayed. As we said, "amen" together, we opened our eyes to find Jasmin standing next to us, staring at us like we'd lost it. "What are you two doing?" she asked.

"Just doing a little asking instead of knocking," Dad said, smiling at me.

Don't forget to flush!

YOUR TURN

- Doors are a physical obstacle; when have you run into an obstacle trying to understand something about faith or God?

- When has something *seemed* like a door, getting in the way of you accomplishing something?

 RUBBING PENCIL LEAD ON THE BARREL OF A SQUEAKY HINGE CAN STOP THE SQUEAK. (BUT ASK A PARENT FIRST.)

68

SOMETHING DAD SAID STUCK IN MY BRAIN and has been rattling around like a BB in a tin can. When we were at the aquarium, he said that asking and knocking was like reaching out in faith. I don't think I really understood the idea at the time, but a funny thing happened to help me get it.

Doors are unpredictable, and sometimes lead to unexpected things. When we went out to eat the other night, I had to run to the bathroom. When I went in, I wasn't thinking of anything except that I needed to go. I pushed open the door on the first stall, and just about jumped out of my skin when someone on the other side shoved the door back closed and yelped unintelligible sounds while I looked closely under the 2nd stall door before going in. I felt bad and tried to apologize. Whoever it was grumbled as he quickly washed up and left the bathroom. On his way out the door, I heard him mumble, "For heaven's sake." Well oddly, that got me thinking about heaven. Which

 TO HALLOW IS "TO MAKE OR SET APART AS HOLY. TO RESPECT OR HONOR GREATLY. TO REVERE."

got me to thinking about our Father in heaven. Probably because Mrs. Johnson is trying to get us to memorize "The Lord's Prayer" at church.

When I looked up the Lord's Prayer in the Bible, guess where it was? Right before the part about asking and knocking! In fact, that whole section in my Bible has a heading that says, "Instruction on Prayer." In Luke 11:2 Jesus is talking and says, *"When you pray, say: 'Father, hallowed be your name, your kingdom come.'"* The way Mrs. Johnson has us learning it is "Our Father, who art in heaven, hallowed be your name. Your kingdom come. Your will be done on earth as it is in heaven." It's a lot more words, but it means the same.

The fact that Jesus tells the disciples how to pray right before he says "knock and it will be opened to you" made me realize that praying is kind of like a doorway for us to go through. Only God is there instead of some grumpy guy. Thank goodness. Don't forget to flush before you go out that door.

YOUR TURN

- **Can you think of times you have used verses in the Bible as a kind of doorway to God?**
- **If the Lord's Prayer is a door for us to go through, do you think there are other ways we can get through the door as well?**
- **Why do you think Jesus gave such a specific prayer to his disciples?**

 KNOCK, KNOCK. WHO'S THERE? DORIS. DORIS WHO? DORIS CLOSED, THAT'S WHY I'M KNOCKING.

69

MY CHURCH GROUP HAD A SPECIAL GET-TOGETHER AT SOMEONE'S HOUSE THE OTHER NIGHT. I love to go to things like that because there are almost always really good snacks and most often some fun games to play. The kids had just gathered together to play "Chubby Bunny" which is where you have an excuse to put as many marshmallows in your mouth as possible. I was certain that I could win.

Then, wouldn't you know it? I had to *go*. I was trying to be quick so I could get back to the marshmallows, but the downstairs bathroom was occupied. Door closed and locked. I really didn't want to tell the world of my dilemma, so I figured I'd see if the hallway stairs led to a solution. As I carefully climbed the stairs, I realized that I was starting to pray. *"Help me not wet my pants, Jesus."* I believe Jesus hears these really important kinds of prayers. Maybe it's strange that I think about prayer and God so often when bathrooms are involved. But surely that's ok. Like a strange good habit.

 THE LONG BEAMS OF LIGHT SHINING THROUGH CLOUDS ARE CALLED CREPUSCULAR RAYS. THEY OCCUR DURING CREPUSCULAR HOURS—AROUND DUSK AND DAWN.

While I climbed, I started thinking about those verses in Luke 11 that talked about Jesus' teaching on prayer. The weirdest ones are at the end of that section. In verses 11-13, Jesus says, *"Which of you fathers, if your son asks for a fish, will give him a snake instead? Or if he asks for an egg, will give him a scorpion? If you then, though you are evil, know how to give good gifts to your children, how much more will your Father in heaven give the Holy Spirit to those who ask him!"*

I wasn't asking for a fish or an egg. Just a toilet with a door that was not closed to me. As I turned at the top of the stairs I almost laughed out loud. Just in front of me was a door wide open with sunset light shining down on an unoccupied bathroom toilet. All that was missing was the singing of angels. It's funny how bathroom doors always seem to be either an obstacle or an opportunity. I said a prayer of thanks as I took care of business before heading back to the game downstairs.

Don't forget to flush!

YOUR TURN

- **What kinds of prayers do you say to God when you're feeling desperate?**
- **When you are given an answer to prayer, do you think of it as a gift? How do you give thanks?**
- **Just for fun, ask a family member what they would give you if you asked for an egg.**

 WHAT IS GOD'S GREATEST GIFT TO US? HIS PRESENCE.

70

I WAS IN THE BATH-ROOM AT SCHOOL THE OTHER DAY.

I was *supposed* to be in the library, but I had to go. I didn't want to walk all the way back to the ones for students, so I snuck into one of the ones for adults up by the front doors of the school. These were always nicer anyway. The stalls were always cleaner, and they didn't have that weird smell that apparently a bunch of kids add to a public bathroom over time.

I decided to stay a while and enjoy myself, so I brought a book. I don't know how much time passed, but suddenly the room plunged into blackness with an audible CLICK. Click? Oh, nuts. The motion sensor

MOTION SENSOR LIGHTS USE INFRARED TECHNOLOGY, WHICH IS SENSITIVE TO THE TEMPERATURE IN THE HUMAN BODY. THE LIGHT TURNS ON WHEN IT DETECTS HUMAN MOVEMENT IN THE ROOM.

lights. I forgot these bathrooms had those so visitors don't just leave the lights on all day. No matter; I shall wave my arms about like a queen in a parade and reactivate them.

WHAT? Still no light? OF COURSE. I'm in a stall. The motion sensors can't see me. I'm trapped, probably forever. This must be how Daniel felt when King Darius tossed him into the den of lions.

Mrs. Johnson told us the story last week. Daniel wanted to pray to God, and some guys that didn't like Daniel tricked the king into making a rule that nobody could pray to anyone but *the king*, as if that makes sense. The punishment for praying was a night in a den of lions. You can read about it in Daniel 6. What was it that King Darius said? Oh right, Daniel 6:16: *"So the king gave the order, and they brought Daniel and threw him into the lions' den. The king said to Daniel, 'May your God, whom you serve continually, rescue you!'"*

Here's hoping I've served God continually enough to be saved from this den of toilets. Don't forget to flush!

YOUR TURN

- **When have you been punished for doing something you thought was *good*?**
- **How do other people see you act when a crisis comes?**

 DANIEL WAS PROBABLY IN HIS EIGHTIES WHEN HE WAS THROWN TO THE LIONS. THAT'S OLD!

71

IT IS UH-MAY-ZING HOW MUCH YOU CAN REMEMBER while sitting in a dark den of toilets. I'm not exactly sure how long I sat there in the teacher's bathroom stall I'd snuck into before the motion sensor light went out, but it was long enough my legs started to tingle. It was SO dark. I could wave my hands wildly trying to be seen by the motion sensor and not even be able to see them.

Because that story about Daniel in the lions' den is pretty cool, I paid close attention and had even re-read it at home a few times. So as I sat in the dark, I started to feel how Daniel might have felt after the king sealed him into the den. I thought about how King Darius spent a sleepless night, and at the first light of day he went to the den to see if Daniel was okay. After all, Daniel had been a well-trusted servant that the king had planned to reward, not punish. When the king called out to see if Daniel was alive, in Daniel 6 verse 21-22 it says,

 PIRATES USED EYE PATCHES TO QUICKLY ADJUST THEIR EYES FROM ABOVE TO BELOW DECK, HAVING ONE EYE TRAINED FOR THE BRIGHT LIGHT AND THE OTHER FOR DIM LIGHT, RESPECTIVELY.

"Daniel answered, 'May the king live forever! My God sent his angel, and he shut the mouths of the lions. They have not hurt me, because I was found innocent in his sight. Nor have I ever done any wrong before you, Your Majesty.'"

I was just remembering how relieved King Darius was when BLAM! On came the lights as the door swooshed opened. Then I heard Jay in a loud whisper, "Eli? Are you in here dude?"

Saved! Light! I don't think I've ever wanted to hug Jay before, but I did give him a big grin as I came out and thanked him while I washed my hands. As we walked out I figured I might not be as innocent as Daniel was, but I was thankful to be saved from an eternity in the den of toilets.

Hmm. Did I flush? Did you? Don't forget!

YOUR TURN

- **Think about a time when you've been in a very dark space. Did you pray for God's protection?**
- **How would you feel if you were Daniel and you were set free after a night with lions?**
- **See if anyone you know has had a bad situation get better after praying.**

 Q: WHAT WOULD YOU CALL A PIRATE WITH FOUR EYES?
A: A PIIIIRATE.

72

I WONDER IF DANIEL EVER GOT PANICKY ABOUT BEING IN THE DARK after his infamous lion's den incident? I know that I have found myself being a little extra vigilant about making sure I don't ever end up stuck in a dark bathroom like before. Have you ever noticed that bathrooms are just about the darkest place when the lights are out? Unless there's a window, of course.

Just yesterday morning, Mom took Jasmin and me out for a special waffle breakfast. When I went into the bathroom to wash my hands, I quickly noticed the lack of windows and that they had one of those motion sensor lights. I found myself washing, and then jumping around waving my hands. Then I put on soap, and then waved around my hands. As quickly as I could, I rinsed and then started waving my hands. The whole time I figured if there was a security camera then someone, somewhere, was cracking up.

 FEAR OF THE DARK IS NYCTOPHOBIA. IN GREEK, NYCTUS MEANS DARKNESS AND PHOBOS MEANS FEAR.

Daniel at least didn't have motion-sensor lights to worry about. AND, after he was pulled out of the lions' den unharmed, King Darius went super-happy crazy. In Daniel 6:26-27 the king said, *"I issue a decree that in every part of my kingdom people must fear and reverence the God of Daniel. For he is the living God and he endures forever; his kingdom will not be destroyed, his dominion will never end. He rescues and he saves; he performs signs and wonders in the heavens and on the earth. He has rescued Daniel from the power of the lions."* I don't have that memorized. I have to look it up each time, but I do go look it up after anytime I start to get freaked out about using a public bathroom whose lights might cut out on me. Then I imagine someone making the decree for me. "Everyone must honor the God of Eli. For he protects from the fear of dark, and he saves Eli from overzealous motion sensor lights from turning off."

It's pretty catchy. Hey—don't forget to flush before turning out the light!

YOUR TURN

- **Why do we feel safer when there is light?**
- **Can you think of a time when God has protected and comforted you?**
- **Do you have any favorite worship songs about God rescuing or saving people?**

 DID YOU HEAR ABOUT THE MONKEY WHO SAT IN A TREE ALL NIGHT WONDERING WHERE THE SUN HAD GONE? THE NEXT MORNING IT DAWNED ON HIM.

73

MY AUNT TERESA HAS A 17-STEP PROCESS FOR GETTING A PUBLIC TOILET CLEAN ENOUGH to do your business that she tried to teach me when I was little. If I have to use a public toilet, I only do an abbreviated version of what she does, but I do generally make sure I'm about to sit on something that I can trust is safe for my booty. The other day I had a classic bad public bathroom experience. Right as I walked through a stall door and saw the not-empty toilet bowl, someone else came in behind me and took the only other stall. Believe me, I thought about just walking out and holding it. But Aunt Teresa's lessons came in handy. Using toilet paper like a biohazard shield, I cleaned the seat and did the ballet move of standing on one foot, using my other to press down on the handle to flush. I don't like loud toilet flushes, but I also don't like a mess. Even if it's not my own. It almost brought tears of thanksgiving to my eyes to see that there were paper seat covers in a box on the wall.

 THE STALL CLOSEST TO THE RESTROOM DOOR CONSISTENTLY HAS THE LOWEST BACTERIA LEVELS (AND THE MOST TOILET PAPER).

Later that day I was reading Isaiah 58 because that's where my Bible fell open to, and Isaiah was fussing at people to do good things for others. I read verses 6-9, but it was verse 8 that had me laughing. It says, *"Then your light will break forth like the dawn, and your healing will quickly appear; then your righteousness will go before you, and the glory of the Lord will be your rear guard."* I've always liked a good Bible verse about dawn breaking forth, but when I saw "the glory of the Lord will be your rear guard," I fell over laughing. That little piece of paper between my rear and the toilet. My rear guard. Ha! That's funny, God. I love it when God cracks me up.

But for real, it's kind of saying God's got my back. Or my backside. I just need to keep doing the good stuff. Hopefully I'll continue having chances to keep doing good stuff. Know what I just realized? I almost never forget to flush when I'm using a public bathroom. I wonder why that is? Don't forget to flush, wherever you are.

YOUR TURN

- When Isaiah said, "your light will break forth like the dawn," what do you think he meant?

- What ways can you do good for others in unexpected places?

- How can you develop a habit of leaving places in better shape than you found them?

Q: WHAT KIND OF TOILET DOES SUPERMAN HAVE?
A: A SUPER BOWL.

74

MY DAD TAKES JASMIN AND ME TO BASEBALL GAMES SOMETIMES ON OUR SUMMER VISITS.

The bathrooms are different than a lot of other places you go. I mean go *to*. In the men's room there's like 25 urinals and for some reason

only like two sit-down toilets. Those two are almost *always* full.

One time when Dad was in there with me, I realized he noticed that I used the sit-down stall without sitting down. When we got back to our seats, he asked me, "Hey bud, you remember last time we were here and we went to get food? All you wanted was a big puffy pretzel. There were two left, and when we got to the counter, the guy in front of us bought them both. Remember?"

Of course I remembered. I had accidentally blurted out, "NO! *I* was getting one of those!" The guy actually made a face at me and said, "Tough luck, kid." Great job being an adult, dude. Crushing the dreams of children.

  TOILETS CONSUME **25** PERCENT OF THE WATER IN YOUR HOME. NOT SURE IF MUTTLEY DRINKING FROM THE TOILET AFFECTS THIS NUMBER.

"On the way home, we talked about the difference between right and wrong and good and better." He opened his Bible app, "Here, Romans 12:2: '*Do not conform to the pattern of this world, but be transformed by the renewing of your mind. Then you will be able to test what God's will is—his good, pleasing and perfect will.*'"

"Oh right, it was good that he got pretzels; it would have been pleasing if he had let me have one," I remembered. "But what about the bathroom?"

"You didn't need a sit-down toilet but used one anyway. There were three guys that looked like they *really* needed one behind you."

"So it was good for *me* to be in there, but more pleasing to God to have let them go instead?" I asked.

"I think so," Dad said. "Did you at least remember to flush?"

I did! Make sure you don't forget to flush too.

YOUR TURN

- **When have you missed an opportunity to put somebody else's needs or wants before yours?**
- **How does it feel when somebody *doesn't* take your feelings into account, whether on purpose or accidentally?**

IN JAPAN, SOME URINALS HAVE VOICE-ACTIVATED FLUSHES. THESE URINALS CAN RESPOND TO AS MANY AS 30 DIFFERENT LANGUAGES!

75

WE'RE OUT FOR A FAMILY DINNER.

It's all of us—Mom, Dad, me, and Jasmin. It's weird and nice all at once. Dad is dropping us back off with Mom, and every now and then we get to all eat together. It's one of those restaurants that's supposed to be famous for its cheeseburgers  but for some reason doesn't have cheeseburgers on the kids' menu. It wouldn't bother me except—

GAAARRRRRROOOOOOOOOOOSSSSHH

Jumping Christmas. I'm in the bathroom, seated, and apparently I'm short enough that if I don't sit *very* still I trigger the auto flush. And it's one of those that's so loud and violent it sounds like it's going to suck all the air out of the room, which scares me to death. Here let me—

GAAARRRRRROOOOOOOOOOOSSSSHH

  THE HARDEST THING TO FLUSH DOWN A TOILET (THAT CAN ACTUALLY FIT DOWN A TOILET) IS A PING-PONG BALL.

See? I kinda feel like even the *toilet* is trying to tell me to hurry up in here. I'll admit I'm starting to see its point. I didn't do a lot of thinking until recently about how long I stay in the bathroom. I would just come in for the obvious reasons, maybe have a quality mind-wander or a couple of good stares at everything, and then remember I should probably leave. But ever since Dad brought the idea of looking out for the interests of others—even strangers—I've been fascinated by making short work of this bathroom thing. I even found my own verse about it, Colossians 4:5: *"Be wise in the way you act toward outsiders; make the most of every opportunity."* The verses around it seem to mean the author was writing about talking about Jesus, but this works too. What if I can start thinking about the feelings of others everywhere, not just in the bathroom? Think of the—

GAAARRRRRROOOOOOOOOOOSSSSHH

Oh right. My family is waiting for me. Gotta scoot. Don't forget to flush!

YOUR TURN

- **What are the things you do sometimes that you'd admit are time-wasters?**
- **What do you feel like is the thing that is the *best* use of your time?**

 EVERY YEAR, TOILETS ARE GIVEN AROUND SEVEN MILLION MOBILE PHONES BY FUMBLY TOILET USERS.

76

I'M IN THE GROCERY STORE BATHROOM. IT'S NOT VERY NICE.

Usually I don't like to go to the bathroom unless it's in a house. With a house bathroom, you get the feeling that *someone* cares about it, even if you can tell they only remembered to care about it right before you arrived. But in public, you get what you get.

Mom is shopping, and I suddenly realize that I have to go *right now*, but I'm not so sure this is such a good idea. Before I came in here, Mom said, "Don't feel like you have to touch the walls," and gave me her phone. What am I gonna do, call the grocery store if there's a problem? This whole place feels distinctly *un*cared for, and it isn't just the weird smell or flickering lights. People have written all over the walls of the stall. At school, I'm used to seeing the occasional "your a pooper" corrected by somebody else to "*you're* a pooper" before a

 THE WORD *GRAFFITI* COMES FROM AN ITALIAN WORD MEANING "A SCRATCH OR SCRIBBLE."

custodian cleans it off the wall of the stall, but this stuff is next level. It's like the royalty of profanity got together for a party, and I shouldn't have been invited. I'm used to reading while I'm in the bathroom, but I feel like I probably shouldn't be reading this. Most of it isn't in complete sentences anyway.

Wait a minute. Right in the middle of a bunch of especially bad words (and subpar illustrations), somebody wrote, "EPH 429." Mom's got a Bible app on her phone—I bet that's Ephesians 4:29. Yep: "*Do not let any unwholesome talk come out of your mouths, but only what is helpful for building others up according to their needs, that it may benefit those who listen.*"

It's so weird to feel *confronted* by reading material. I'm not offended; Dad talked me through most of these words when I was younger so I'd know they're really just words—words I *don't* use. I just wonder what's going on in all these people's lives that *this* is how they express themselves.

YOUR TURN

- **When have you been surprised by the way other people choose to talk?**
- **How do you decide what kind of words you'll read or use around your family? What about around friends?**
- **Don't forget to flush!**

IN TEXAS, A HIGH SCHOOL STUDENT WAS PUT IN JAIL FOR WRITING HIS BAND'S NAME IN A BATHROOM STALL.

77

READING SUCH UGLY STUFF ON THE BATHROOM WALL IN THE GROCERY STORE made me feel like I got poked in the eye. I didn't ask for it, but it couldn't be undone. Both my mom and dad have talked to Jasmin and me about trying to be *careful little eyes what we see*. Their favorite thing to say is that you can't *unsee* stuff. That's easier to guard against if you just stay at home or visit only places you know are "safe." But since that's hard to do, I've been hoping to at least only go places where the bathroom walls are clean. *Word* clean, not just dirt clean.

I even prayed about it and read further in Ephesians than just 4:29. I decided that Ephesians 4:31-32 would probably be good verses to memorize. They say, *"Get rid of all bitterness, rage and anger, brawling and slander, along with every form of malice. Be kind and*

 GRAFFITI WAS FIRST FOUND ON ANCIENT ROMAN ARCHITECTURE.

compassionate to one another, forgiving each other, just as in Christ God forgave you." Can you imagine what the world would be like if we could just do these two verses?

That's why I've been trying to think of ways I can combat bad bathroom writing when we're out and about. I figure there's got to be a way to have kindness win out on walls. But it's tricky since you also don't want to actually *write* on the walls. Because that's it's own kind of not okay. For right now, I'm going back to my old stand-by tool—sticky notes!

While we were out today, I've put up two sticky notes with "Ephesians 4:31-32" written on them. Well, I put up one and had Jasmin put one up in the girl's bathroom at the bank. That way, we figure that if someone wants to, they can take the sticky note with them and look it up at home. Tidy and positive. You can help out by not forgetting to flush!

YOUR TURN

- Can you think of other ways that all the ugliness in verse 31 can be overcome by the goodness in verse 32?
- Have you ever gone on a campaign to take kindness and forgiveness into the world?
- Was there a time you needed forgiveness from someone and got it? How did that feel?

 POOP JOKES MIGHT NOT BE IN YOUR HUMOR TOP FIVE, BUT FOR ME THEY'RE A SOLID NUMBER TWO.

78

SHHH! Okay, I'm really just shushing myself. Today I'm being dragged around on errands with Aunt Teresa, and she had to get a "quick hair cut." I knew when she said it that, there could be no such thing. But still I had hoped. After reading through every ladies magazine on the tables in the waiting area

and then laying my head over the back of my seat and staring at the lights until my eyes began to twitch, I headed to the bathroom—more out of boredom than any actual need. There was stuff everywhere! Shelves with tiny figurines of cats, a shelf with more magazines, and even a little New Testament people hand out sometimes. Little bowls of stuff Mom calls potpourri. It looks like pinecones, wood shavings and acorns made into a salad, but it smells like a perfume factory testing ground. More argument against salad.

I was just realizing that I forgot to bring my sticky notes with me to add a new bathroom to my list of places conquered with kindness. That's

160

I USED TO NOT LIKE MY HAIR. THEN IT GREW ON ME.

when my laugh burst out like a hyena with bronchitis. I noticed the little sign over the toilet. It read: "I hope your day is as nice as your butt."

"Aaaahhhhaaaaa ha ha!"

"Eli, are you ok in there?" I heard Aunt Teresa calling from the chair she was trapped in for her haircut.

"I'm fine, Aunt Teresa!" I snickered, more in control now. Well now. That was funny. It was kind of like hair salon graffiti I guess. I decided that I'd open the little New Testament to Ephesians and leave it out. When I got close to Ephesians 4, though, I noticed Ephesians 5:4 first. It said, *"Nor should there be obscenity, foolish talk or coarse joking, which are out of place, but rather thanksgiving."* I put a square of toilet paper under that verse so someone after me would see it.

Then I walked out of there giving thanks for funny that wasn't foul or dirty. Funny *and* positive! Don't forget to flush before you walk out.

YOUR TURN

- **What kinds of signs can you imagine seeing in places that would bring humor and thankfulness?**
- **Why do you think Paul encouraged the Ephesians so much in sharing kindness and thanksgiving?**
- **Make an encouraging, maybe even funny, note that you can leave for someone you care about.**

 Q: HOW DOES THE MAN IN THE MOON CUT HIS HAIR?
A: ECLIPSE IT!

79

WHY IS IT THAT WHEN I'M IN PUBLIC, I only realize I need to go to the bathroom when it's escalated to an emergency?

I barely made it. It's Taco Tuesday at school today. My friends and I sometimes call it Tac-*GO* Tuesday due to the way it eventually becomes gastronomically insistent. I ran here straight from science. We're working on group projects and we were allowed to choose *whatever topic we wanted.* For some reason our group said, "Species of amphibians!" We thought two things about amphibians: 1) "Amphibians" sounds funny, and 2) Amphibians are people that can do things with either hand.

We were correct about number one. But number two we got wrong. (Heh, heh. I said, "number two.") People that can do things with both hands are *ambidextrous.* Amphibians are frogs, toads, newts, sala-manders . . . and so on. It turns out there are OVER SIX THOUSAND species of amphibians. HOW ARE WE GOING TO DO THIS?

 MOST AMPHIBIANS START OUT WITH GILLS AND TAILS, NOT LEGS AND LUNGS. GO AHEAD AND FREAK OUT ABOUT THAT A LITTLE.

I told Mom about it last night, and she said it sounded like we didn't plan our tower very well. "Just tell me the Bible story, Mom," I said. It's *always* a Bible story when she says something weird like that. She read me Luke 14:28: *"Suppose one of you wants to build a tower. Won't you first sit down and estimate the cost to see if you have enough money to complete it?"*

"I'm not trying to build a tower, Mom," I said, but she just smiled. Sitting here now I think I know what she means. If I'd looked up how many species of amphibians there are—or even what an amphibian *is*—I could have saved my group a lot of trouble. I should have paid attention. I should have thought ahead.

OH. NO. It appears that I have once again failed to estimate materials. I just reached for the TP—I got cardboard tube again. I'll catch you later. Hey, plan ahead to when you walk out of here: don't forget to flush.

YOUR TURN

- **When have you rushed ahead on something, only to have it affect others later?**
- **When has simply not paying attention caused you trouble?**
- **What about following Jesus might cost you socially?**

 Q: WHY DID THE FROG GET IN TROUBLE FOR CHEATING AT SCHOOL?
A: SOMEBODY TOAD ON HIM.

80

I THINK THERE IS SOMETHING TERRIBLY WRONG WITH ME. This is not the first time I've dreamt about toilet paper. Maybe it won't be my last. But it does make me wonder about myself. I'm an okay kid. I mean, I'm not perfect, but I pretty much stay on the good side of the law. But I can't help what I dream, can I?

In my dream I was a king, but for some reason I was sitting on a throne in the school bathroom, staring into the janitor's closet counting rolls of ammo. Err . . . well, toilet paper. And although I couldn't see him, I knew that there was another king in another bathroom doing the same thing. We were going to have an all out TP rolling war, and I was trying to make sure we had enough, uh, ammo. All my friends were waiting nervously behind me because they were worried we didn't have enough. Which we didn't. I knew it because I'd finished counting. In a dreamy and regal way, I stood up and faced my friends. And that's when I woke up standing in the middle of my bed with my blankets draped around me.

 Q: WHERE DO KINGS AND QUEENS GET CROWNED?
A: ON THE HEAD!

You see, after the verses about counting the cost of making a tower that mom brought up, Luke 14:31-33 is another mini one-liner parable about a king. It says, *"Or suppose a king is about to go to war against another king. Won't he first sit down and consider whether he is able with ten thousand men to oppose the one coming against him with twenty thousand? If he is not able, he will send a delegation while the other is still a long way off and will ask for terms of peace. In the same way, those of you who do not give up everything you have cannot be my disciples."*

It's Jesus talking again about the need to count the cost of choosing a path and hoping you'll choose the path of a disciple. Now when I see the door to the janitor closet in the bathroom at school, I find myself wondering who I should make peace with. It's kind of crazy, but don't let it distract you from flushing.

YOUR TURN

- How do you think things would turn out if the king didn't consider the cost in that situation?
- Why do you think Jesus wants people to count the cost of becoming a follower?
- Go and ask a family member if they have a favorite parable.

Q: WHERE DOES A KING KEEP HIS ARMIES?
A: UP HIS SLEEVIES.

81

AFTER THE TOWER AND KING PARABLES IN LUKE 14 that Jesus uses to talk about the cost of being a disciple, there's another one that mentions manure. Jesus is clearly not afraid to talk about poo. If you think about it, poo is a holy opportunity for a really interesting conversation starter.

It came in handy the other day at church. I had gone into the bathroom and was sitting in my own private thinking stall, pondering the importance of Jesus' words about manure. I knew someone had come in to the stall next to me, but I wasn't really paying attention. That is, until I heard a sigh and then a hesitant question. "I don't suppose you could pass me some toilet paper, could you?" I knew the feeling. So in an attempt to lighten the awkward mood I said, "Sure! There's an extra roll in here." I was using my God-given usefulness! As I handed the roll under I decided I should volunteer some of my vast collection of biblical knowledge, too.

 MANY PEOPLE AROUND THE WORLD USE WATER AFTER USING THE TOILET, INSTEAD OF TOILET PAPER.

"You know, it's funny—I was just thinking about the fact that even Jesus spoke about poo. I was reading Luke 14:34 and 35 just this morning where Jesus said, *'Salt is good, but if it loses its saltiness, how can it be made salty again? It is fit neither for the soil nor for the manure pile; it is thrown out. Whoever has ears to hear, let them hear.'*"

Whew. I was so proud that I'd remembered the whole thing. Then I noticed the absolute silence. "Um . . . I like the poo reference, but . . . what?" More silence. Wow. Talk about considering the cost of being a disciple. Awkward and uncomfortable can really add up when reaching out to strangers who need toilet paper.

After a gentle clearing of his throat, he suggested, "Well, I guess we should make sure we stay salty, huh?" Relief swam through me. "Yeah. That's just what I was thinking too." I heard the sound of flushing (don't forget!) and hand washing. And just as he walked out the door, I heard him say, "I guess having ears is a big responsibility." I don't know who he was, but I felt like he got me.

YOUR TURN

- **How many times have you felt awkward when trying to be helpful to someone?**

- **If you are trying to be useful and helpful to others, how could that be a cost of discipleship?**

 PLANTS NEED SALT TO THRIVE, BUT TOO MUCH SALT CAN KILL THEM. THIS IS CALLED "OVERSALINIZATION."

82

SOMETIMES I THINK LIFE IS LEARNING ONE THING JUST IN TIME TO REALIZE YOU DON'T KNOW SOMETHING ELSE.

I'm in the school bathroom. It's not a normal bathroom break time. If I can just be honest here—I hate pooping with other people in a public bathroom. I mean, sure, you're in a stall, but that only takes care of the sense of *sight*, if you follow my reasoning. I don't want to *hear* somebody else do that, and I try to return the favor. So if I *must* do that during the day, I wait and excuse myself from class.

This time being alone backfired on me. (Stop it; that's not a joke.) When I finished, I flushed—and the terror began: not quite the right flushy noises, water coming up instead of going down, full engagement of fight-or-flight in my sympathetic nervous system. Fortunately it stopped before it got to the rim, but now I've got a situation. *I know*

 THE CLEANEST STALL IN THE BATHROOM IS USUALLY THE FIRST, BECAUSE IT'S USUALLY THE LEAST USED.

how to fix this, but THERE'S NO PLUNGER IN HERE. I'm trying to grow up, I swear. But I keep doing things that make grownups sigh at me like I'm just a dumb kid.

Last month we had Youth Sunday at church. Our theme verse was 1 Timothy 4:12: *"Don't let anyone look down on you because you are young, but set an example for the believers in speech, in conduct, in love, in faith and in purity."* I can't prove it, but I think they use that verse every year for Youth Sunday. I liked it though, because it talks about a lot of what I've been trying to do, especially when I'm around adults.

Yet here I am with a toilet full of troubles and bubbles. I guess I could have looked around to see if there was a plunger before I started, but who wants to go through life assuming the worst-case scenario is going to happen?

I've got to focus. I'm smart enough to handle this. You focus too— don't forget to flush.

YOUR TURN

- **When have you had to rise above a situation—whether you created it or not?**
- **How do you approach adults when you need help with a problem they don't know about yet?**

 IN ROME, PIPES WERE ORIGINALLY MADE FROM LEAD, WHICH IS "PLUMBUM" IN LATIN. A PERSON WHO WORKED WITH LEAD WAS CALLED A PLUMBARIUS.

83

YES, I'M STILL STANDING IN FRONT OF THIS VERY FULL TOILET.

Yes, the bell is about to ring. Yes, there's about to be a million people in here. The very next verse after our Youth Sunday theme verse is 1 Timothy 4:13, and it says, *"Until I come, devote yourself to the public reading of Scripture, to preaching and to teaching."*

No, I don't think Jesus is coming to bring me a plunger, and no, I'm not going to try to preach my way out of this. But I had that verse in my head a couple of weeks ago in a sort of similar situation. We were out for fast food, and when I went to the bathroom, the door banged into something before I could get it all the way open. I squeezed around it, and discovered the bathroom door had banged into the stall door (why do fast-food restaurants have tiny bathrooms sometimes?). The stall door was blocked open by a kid a couple of years older than me in a wheelchair. He was a little red-faced and looked embarrassed.

"I stopped up the toilet," he said. "I'm pretty new to this wheelchair, and I wasn't very good at plunging even before I got hurt playing baseball. Any chance you can help me?"

Now you might be thinking, "What a horrific, disgusting mess," and you'd partially be right. But all *I* was thinking was, "a chance to shine, this time without ruining socks." I could teach him. He might not be able to actually *do* it until his injury healed, but I could teach him—devoting myself to it, so to speak. If it went wrong, he could probably roll away faster than me anyway.

It went perfectly. My confidence in myself is restored. Now, to deal with this toilet at school. I'll keep you posted. Don't forget to flush.

YOUR TURN

- **How do memories of past successes help you when you're trying to lead or teach a friend or group something?**

- **How do your mistakes over time sometimes build into an eventual success?**

WORLD TOILET DAY IS NOVEMBER 19. MAKE SURE YOUR TOILET IS CLEAN ON THAT DAY AND LEARN ABOUT ACCESS TO CLEAN TOILETS AROUND THE WORLD.

84

GAME FACE. TIME TO SHOW THIS TOILET WHO IS BOSS.

I'm the toilet boss, that's who. I'm counting on the final verse from the Youth Sunday bulletin for confidence. 1 Timothy 4:15 says, *"Be diligent in these matters; give yourself wholly to them, so that everyone may see your progress."* This is my moment. I shall hold my progress high, like a victory banner, leading me into—

"Hey, Mr. Steve. MR. STEVE." I'm speed-walking down the school hallway after our building maintenance supervisor. I don't know his last name; we just all call him Mr. Steve. "Mr. Steve!" I finally catch up to him. In a long rambling, run-on sentence I'll spare you here, I explained at length the nature of the problem and my willingness and ability to fix it myself apart from the lack of appropriate tools, namely, a plunger. He looked bemusedly at me until I finished. "The bathroom by the library? Don't worry about it. I'll fix it."

Q: WHAT DID THE JANITOR SAY WHEN HE JUMPED OUT OF HIS STORAGE ROOM? A: SUPPLIES!

"But I wanted to show my progress," I stammered.

That stopped him in his tracks. "What?" he asked. I explained about the verse. He patted me on the shoulder. "I appreciate it, kid, but you've already shown me progress. You're the only kid that's ever come to me and admitted that *they* stopped up the toilet. If I'm lucky, somebody comes and says they 'found it.' Nobody ever confesses. You did good. It means a lot to me, actually."

"Are you sure?" I asked, still willing, but beginning to feel relief.

"Yup." He started to move on. "Anyway, I'm pretty sure there's a rule about not asking kids to go near poop, even if it's their own."

Fair enough. Drama concluded. Don't forget to flush!

- **When have you stepped up to a situation where you felt underprepared or knew you needed things that weren't there?**
- **How do you gain confidence in those times?**
- **Who does it mean the most to you to see you succeed?**

SOME CHURCHES EMPLOY A SEXTON, OR CARETAKER. IT COMES FROM THE LATIN WORD *SACRISTANUS* MEANING "CUSTODIAN OF SACRED OBJECTS."

85

WHEN YOU'RE REALLY LITTLE, you can just play in the same clothes all day. But when you get older, sometimes you have to "dress out" for PE. To be honest, I had kind of always wanted to be in a locker room, but the reality of it is a little intimidating at first. I don't think it would have been quite

so bad if everybody had just been chill about it. But some kids like to cover up nerves and act big by making other kids feel small.

Our locker room has a row of shower stalls with a plastic curtain hanging down. If you want privacy, you use one of these, but you either have to be quick or sometimes wait. I was just pulling up my shorts one day and thinking how crazy brave you'd have to be in order to actually take a shower in one of these stalls when I heard Jay causing a ruckus on the other side of the curtain. Next thing I know, he's whipping open my curtain and saying, "Come on shower hog.

Q: WHY DID THE TOMATO BLUSH?
A: BECAUSE HE SAW THE SALAD DRESSING.

Get outta here and make room." I wasted no time getting out of his way.

It bothered me, though. I went home thinking about it and kind of hoped I could find some heavenly guidance for such an earthly problem. In a letter to people living in hostile places, 1 Peter had some good things to say. In 1 Peter 5:6-7 it says, *"Humble yourselves, therefore, under God's mighty hand, that he may lift you up in due time. Cast all your anxiety on him because he cares for you."*

I figured that was a pretty good word. I remember talking to Dad about it too. He suggested that I try to remember to pray for Jay. That seemed pretty humble, so I did. Jay eventually settled down when it came time to use the locker room, and at the same time I kind of had a different attitude about him. Still don't have any plans to actually shower there though. Enjoy your alone time, and don't forget to flush!

YOUR TURN

- **What types of situations cause you a lot of anxiety or fear?**
- **What do you think it means to "humble yourself under God's mighty hand"?**
- **Go find an adult and ask about ways they humble themselves.**

TIPS FOR CHANGING IN A LOCKER ROOM: BE EARLY TO CHANGE. BE QUICK. SHOW RESPECT TO OTHERS.

86

LAST SUMMER I WENT WITH MY CHURCH TO CAMP.
I'd been on overnight trips before, but this was my first time away from both of my parents at the same time for most of a week.

So it came down to the last night of camp, and my whole cabin realized that none of us had taken showers all week. Also, none of us wanted to be packed in a church van the way we smelled. We grabbed our gear and ran to the camp bathhouse. If any of us had showered earlier in the week we'd have known it already, but there were four showers and NO CURTAINS. (Alarm.)

Our theme verse for the week was Galatians 6:2, which says, *"Carry each other's burdens, and in this way you will fulfill the law of Christ."* All week long we'd been talking through dozens of ways we could "look out for the little guy" and "put others first" and stuff like that. Here, at 10:45 p.m. on the last night of camp, we seemed to have stumbled

Q: WHAT GETS WETTER AND WETTER THE MORE IT DRIES?
A: A TOWEL. TRY TO PAY ATTENTION. WE ALREADY TOLD YOU THIS.

into some sort of team-building exercise. Or maybe something like a final exam for camp. We suddenly had a very similar burden to share: trying to get clean without showing everyone our bottoms.

The plan actually came together pretty quickly; it took four of us to let a fifth person take a shower. Two of us held a towel high and two held a towel low, forming an impromptu shower curtain. The whole thing was a perfect exercise in humility—we had to put the privacy of the others above our own desire to just be in bed, and it was humbling to have four friends serving as my shower curtain when it was my turn.

It wasn't a perfect plan. We ended up not getting back to our cabin until an hour after lights out, and it turns out that if you use your towel as a shower curtain it gets too wet to use it as a towel. I bet we never forget that shower, though. Don't forget to flush!

YOUR TURN

- **When have you really been humble—a time when you put someone's needs ahead of yours?**
- **What examples of humility have you seen in others?**

 Q: WHAT'S THE BEST WAY TO GET A BABY CLEAN?
A: BABY SHOWER.

87

THE DRIVE HOME FROM CAMP WAS TOO LONG TO DO IN ONE DAY—or at least longer than the driver wanted to spend with kids in a church van in a single day. We were told that the hotel we stayed in was "nicer than where we'd usually stay on a church trip," so we had to be on our best behavior. It didn't seem *all* that

nice, but they at least had a waffle maker in the lobby. My roommates and I were just deciding if it was possible to do a front flip from one bed onto the other without hitting the ceiling when somebody knocked on the door. All of our friends were in the hall. "You have to come see Taylor's shower," someone said.

We all herded down to Taylor's room. His was on the end of the hall, and it was bigger than an apartment. "You got a *suite*," somebody who stays in more hotels than me said. "I'll show you what's sweet," Taylor replied (using a homophone) and led us into his bathroom.

STUDIES SHOW THAT 43,000 CHILDREN ARE INJURED EVERY YEAR IN THE SHOWER. BE CAREFUL OUT THERE.

Sweet Moses. Glass. Tile. Eight shower heads, all of them with different jobs. It had a "steam" button that made it fill up with steam so thick you couldn't see. It was amazing, and I don't even like to shower all that much.

"Alright, get out. And I'm gonna need to crash on one of your rooms' floor," said Taylor.

"What?" we all said at the same time.

"I'm giving it to Mr. Lee," he answered. Mr. Lee was our driver and had been with us all week. "He's exhausted, and the air conditioner is broken in his room. He needs it more than me."

It *did* seem like the right thing to do, but it was still surprising. I'd have been so excited about the fancy room I might have forgotten there was anyone else on the trip. Taylor said a phrase from one of our devotions during the week had jumped into his head when he heard Mr. Lee's A/C was out: Acts 2:44-45 says, *"All the believers were together and had everything in common. They sold property and possessions to give to anyone who had need."*

YOUR TURN

- **When have you realized that you missed an opportunity to give something up for somebody else?**
- **In what other ways can you try to show more humility?**

 THE WORDS *SHAMPOO* AND *PAJAMAS* REPORTEDLY COME TO US FROM INDIA.

88

I'VE BEEN PRETTY OPEN ABOUT THE FACT THAT MY "FRIEND" JAY FROM SCHOOL KEEPS ME A LITTLE ON EDGE. I don't know if he's exactly a textbook *bully*, but he'd give you a good idea of what to look for if you needed one. Ever since I decided to pray for him recently, it's been interesting to think of him differently than before. Still, I was pretty surprised when he handed me an invitation to his birthday party sleepover. And I was even more surprised when Mom said I could go. She knows his parents and says that it will be a good time to get to know him better. It's been a lot to digest in a short time.

I had almost everything packed a little while ago, but when I went to grab the tube of toothpaste, Jasmin started squawking about it being her toothpaste. It seems she's forgotten the fact that over the many years she's had teeth, we've both shared the same tube. When I went to get Mom's support, she didn't seem worried. She said, "You'll be just like one of those that Jesus sent out who had to depend on

 EXPERTS BELIEVE THAT THE FIRST TOOTHPASTES ORIGINATED IN INDIA, EGYPT, AND CHINA AROUND 5000 BCE.

others. I'm sure Jay will have toothpaste you can use." I didn't care for it as a plan. But it got me curious. After wondering where in the Bible Jesus did such a thing, I of course had to go look it up.

In Luke 10, Jesus decided to send 72 people to go out before him. In verses 3 and 4, it clearly states, *"Go! I am sending you out like lambs among wolves. Do not take a purse or bag or sandals; and do not greet anyone on the road."* It sounded a little more dire than just heading for a sleepover without toothpaste, but it was an interesting challenge. They had to depend on total strangers for everything! And they were in a hurry. All I have to do is depend on the parents of my some-times-nemesis to give me a little toothpaste. I think I can handle it.

"ELI! Come on now, we're in a hurry!"

That's Mom. Wish me luck, and don't forget to flush.

YOUR TURN

- **Have you ever forgotten to pack something important and had to ask for it as a guest?**
- **What would your response be if someone visiting your home was in need of something?**
- **Think of some basics that you could keep on hand or even donate to people in need. See what you can gather.**

 THE ROMANS USED TO PUT URINE IN THEIR TOOTHPASTE BECAUSE URINE CONTAINS AMMONIA, A GOOD CLEANSER.

89

I'M A DEAD MAN.

Much to my surprise, Jay *did* loan me his toothpaste. It wasn't even some kind of trick toothpaste that tastes like soap (I checked before brushing). Now, however, I have spurned the only kindness he has ever offered me— I dropped the lid to his toothpaste down his sink drain.

I've done it plenty of times at my house, but ours has a little plug in the drain that stops things from going down. Jay's plug is missing, and now his toothpaste cap is missing, too. Dead, dead, dead. I guess I had a good run. Tell my family I loved them . . .

BAM! "Are you coming out?" Jay already did not sound amused. "Jusaminnit," I mumbled. I was so worried about the cap I'd forgotten to spit out the toothpaste. What to do what to do what to do. Wait, what did the disciples do? In Luke 10, Jesus sent them out with

CONTACTS, JEWELRY, AND TOOTHPASTE CAPS ARE AMONG THE MOST COMMON ITEMS DROPPED DOWN A SINK DRAIN.

nothing, and Jasmin had joked me out the door without toothpaste over it. When the disciples got somewhere, they were supposed to . . . offer it peace! Luke 10:5 says, *"When you enter a house, first say, 'Peace to this house.'"* Peace was all the disciples had to offer; they'd left everything else behind, totally relying on strangers to provide.

This is a different kind of reliance than I've ever even heard of. When I walk out that door, I'm relying on the very person I've offended to let me off the hook. I'm going to do a little praying for peace in this house before I go. Before you walk out your door, don't forget to flush. And don't forget to brush, if it's that time of day.

YOUR TURN

- **When have you had to tell someone something difficult?**
- **How did you rely on God in that moment?**

TOOTHPASTE: "SOMETIMES I FEEL LIKE I HAVE THE WORST JOB IN THE WORLD." TOILET PAPER: "WHATEVER, BUDDY."

90

I CHICKENED OUT.

After dropping the cap down the drain, I just couldn't bring myself to tell Jay. I was the last one to use the bathroom, so I just stuck the open tube behind the tissue paper box they keep on their counter. I figured this would buy me seven to ten hours to figure out a way to bring it up. Or escape.

Lying here in my sleeping bag, I'm still thinking about those disciples. How scary would that be, to just walk around with *nothing*, hoping strangers would take care of you? Jesus did give them instructions for what to do if a town didn't welcome them. In Luke 10:10-11 it says, *"But when you enter a town and are not welcomed, go into its streets and say, 'Even the dust of your town we wipe from our feet as a warning to you. Yet be sure of this: The kingdom of God has come near.'"* Zinger. Good *day*, sir.

 MODERN TOOTHPASTE WAS FIRST INVENTED IN 1780, EVEN THOUGH THAT DOESN'T SOUND VERY MODERN.

Wouldn't it have been hard to walk away, though? I mean, wouldn't you still want a drink of water if the person giving it to you was grouchy about it but eventually sort of willing? Thinking about the word *grouchy* brought my mind back to Jay. I feel like I kinda need to find out how he'll respond without being sneaky about it. Just come right out and ask. If he blows up, he blows up. So be it. At least then I'll know if I need to dust off my sandals, so to speak.

"Pssst, Jay. You awake?" I whisper-hollered.

"No," he whispered back. Interesting approach.

"When I brushed my teeth earlier, I accidentally dropped the cap of your toothpaste down the drain," I offered, nervously. There was a distinct pause.

"I don't care," he said. "I'll put it in a Zip-lock in the morning. Shut up."

That was easier than I expected. Hey, I'm going to sleep. Don't forget to flush.

YOUR TURN

- **When have you been surprised—good or bad—about someone's response to bad news?**
- **How do you know which friends you can rely on, and which ones you can't?**

 FLOURIDE, NATURE'S CAVITY FIGHTER, WAS FIRST ADDED TO TOOTHPASTE IN 1956.

91

I DON'T KNOW WHAT IT IS ABOUT ME AND TOWELS, but I can just about guarantee that when I'm out somewhere and have to wash my hands, there are not going to be any paper towels or towels of any other kind. I almost always come out of a school or store bathroom shaking my hands and then doing the wipe dry on my shirt or pants. Mom

says she's pretty sure that undoes the washing that I just did. It's okay. I figure it's good for the environment to shake dry. I once saw a whole video about how to use fewer paper towels when washing hands out in public.

When I was making do with a good shake at the library the other day, one of the ladies who works there saw me and showed me the secret supply closet for paper towels. She said, "Now you'll know

Q: WHAT DO YOU CALL THE SLEEPY RELATIVE OF A PAPER TOWEL?
A: A NAPKIN.

they're here even if you don't see them." When I said, "Kinda like God, huh?" She smiled and said, "Absolutely."

With that rattling around in my head, I started thinking about one of my favorite psalms. It may be strange to have a favorite, but if you read it, you'll like it too. It's all about you. Verses seven and eight say, *"Where can I go from your Spirit? Where can I flee from your presence? If I go up to the heavens, you are there; if I make my bed in the depths, you are there."* There are all kinds of places in the Bible where it says God is always present around us, but like I said—this is a favorite. Maybe it's strange that something as simple as paper towels in the bathroom can make me think of God's presence. I'm okay with strange. How about you? Hey—don't forget to flush.

YOUR TURN

- **Can you think of something simple that you come across every day that can be a reminder to you of God's presence?**

- **How do you feel knowing that no matter where you go, God will be with you?**

- **Look around you. Is there a towel you can use to dry your hands? Give thanks while doing that after washing up.**

 SOME HAND DRYERS SPREAD 1300 TIMES AS MANY GERMS AROUND THE BATHROOM AS DRYING WITH A PAPER TOWEL.

92

I PLAYED IT PRETTY COOL when I told you about staying in the hotel on the way back from camp, but I was pretty excited about that. I really don't get to stay in hotels all that often and it always feels so . . . luxurious, I guess. My favorite part about staying in a hotel is the way stuff mysteriously appears,

as if from nowhere. Wake up in the morning and the lobby is full of breakfast. Come back to the room at the end of the day and *someone made the beds* and brand new towels are in the bathroom. You get a warm feeling like there's an invisible something looking out for you, providing even when you least expect it. Like a helper.

These days you get to send secret messages to the helpers. In some hotels you can signal to them that you need a new towel by leaving the old one in the floor (I've been trying for years to implement this system at home). But if you're cool with the towel you have and want

 THE AVERAGE COST OF A NIGHT IN A UNITED STATES HOTEL IS OVER $120. THAT'S A LOT OF BIRTHDAY-CARD MONEY.

to look out for the environment by saving washing machine water, you can send *that* signal by hanging the old one back up.

We were only staying one night anyway, but I was happy just remembering that idea of provision lingering in the background like an unseen presence. It makes me think of the way God's spirit was there in the background at creation, right before all the cool stuff happened. Genesis 1:2 says, *"Now the earth was formless and empty, darkness was over the surface of the deep, and the Spirit of God was hovering over the waters."* Hovering! I forgot it actually says *hovering*. How awesome. I think maybe the awesomest thing about God's presence is that it's been there since *before* the beginning. Talk about showing up on time.

Hey, if you're done in here, don't forget to flush. And maybe go thank somebody for being present for you.

YOUR TURN

- **What makes you notice God's presence in your life? Things in nature? Maybe other people?**
- **Who are the people that provide the most for you?**
- **How can you be a welcome presence in the lives of others?**

 MORE THAN 15 MILLION PEOPLE ARE EMPLOYED BY HOTELS IN THE UNITED STATES ALONE. THAT'S A LOT OF HELPERS.

93

WE'D ALL PRETTY
WELL HAD IT WITH THE
CHURCH VAN ON THE
SECOND DAY OF OUR
DRIVE. Matt, our driver,
made one last bathroom
stop at a highway rest
area because he said the
church would be locked
when we got back. After
I used the bathroom, I
washed my hands and
then stood there looking
around with my hands
dribbling water all over the

floor. Where are the *towels*? Why does this always happen to me?!
I only wash my hands because it makes Mom happy, and she's not
even here. Every single time I'm out in public I–

WHAAAAAAAAOOOOOOOOOOOSSSSSSSSSHHHHHHHHH

I protectively ducked and covered my head, getting water in one
of my ears. The noise reminded me of when a hole gets ripped in
a plane in the movies, and all those yellow mask things drop down
while everybody screams and waves their hands.

  AUTOMATIC HAND DRYERS HAVE SIGNIFICANTLY LESS IMPACT ON THE
ENVIRONMENT THAN USING PAPER TOWELS.

"Sorry kid. Never seen one of these?" said a stranger. I finally realized the noise had come from a hand dryer. And *what* a hand dryer! I braced for the noise and stuck my hands under it. The roar returned, and the air hit my hands so powerfully it made an indention in my skin. This thing could take off a birthmark.

I mentioned it when I got back in the van. Matt said when he first saw one it made him think of when God's Spirit showed up at Pentecost. He told one of us to read from Acts 2. In verse two it says, *"Suddenly a sound like the blowing of a violent wind came from heaven and filled the whole house where they were sitting."* What an appearance! Jesus' disciples had gathered, waiting for whatever was next. God's presence was next! I'd read that story before but never really paid attention to the *noise level* God apparently creates upon arrival. They had to know something big was about to happen in their lives!

Speaking of noise level . . . never mind, I was going to be gross. Just don't forget to flush, OK?

YOUR TURN

- **When have you felt God's presence? Where were you?**
- **How do you make your presence known when you arrive?**
- **How has God's presence changed how you live?**

 THE FIRST AIR-DRYING HAND DRYER WAS PATENTED UNDER THE NAME "AIRDRY THE ELECTRIC TOWEL." CATCHY.

94

YEP. THAT'S A HUMDINGER. I'm supposed to be in math class, but instead I'm in the bathroom, staring in the mirror at what looks like a fluffy surrender flag coming from the back of my head. My hair is reaching for the sky. As I wet my hand and try to slick it down, I see my scowl reflected back at me while I think back to a few minutes ago.

As I walked down the hall, there was Jay headed right for me. Walking past, he reached up and rubbed his hand in my hair like he was trying to smear a cream pie on top of my head. As he walked on past, he said (loudly) over his shoulder, "Dude! You've got a serious case of bed head. You should do something about that!" So now I'm rubbing my wet paw through my hair like a cat, having a full-blown daydream about how good it would have felt to snap back with a

Q: WHAT DO YOU CALL A BEE HAVING A BAD HAIR DAY?
A: A FRISBEE!

quick (and loud) "Why don't you go fix your own feathers, Blue Jay!" Only that would probably have ruined whatever this friend thing is we've started.

Instead I kept remembering his blast of hallway judgment, and looked up Matthew 7 when I got home—I remembered it being something about judging people. I got a little excited when I read to verse five where Jesus called names. He said "You hypocrite!" Heh, heh. Not sure what that means, but it sounds like a sweet ka-pow to use on somebody. *"First take the plank out of your own eye, and then you will see clearly to remove the speck from your brother's eye."* It would be nice if these verses were just speaking to *Jay*. I'm pretty glad I didn't bust out my slam on Jay. If I see him with bed head someday, I'd like to think I'll only be understanding, but you never know. We'll see. It happens to everyone.

Don't forget to flush. Oh, and check your hair too.

YOUR TURN

- Have you ever realized something in the Bible that you thought was about *others* is actually something *you* should be thinking about?
- Have you ever had a friend embarrass you in front of others? Or wanted to do it right back? How do these verses speak to you?

 THE TERM "COW LICK" IS CALLED THAT BECAUSE IT LOOKS AS IF IT WAS PRODUCED BY A LICK FROM A PASSING COW.

95

JAY'S GONNA GET IT NOW.

I re-read those verses from Matthew 7 a few times last night, and finally the first verse jumped out at me. Matthew 7:1 says, *"Do not judge, or you too will be judged."* Plain and simple.

Vindication! The Bible says I can make fun of Jay today. He judged my appearance; today I will judge his. Can't argue with Jesus.

I spent the ride to school thinking up good one-liners to burn him with. Something about his hair would be appropriate—that's exactly what he did to me. Or maybe something about his clothes. People seem to get sensitive about their clothes. Would something about his *face* be too far? I mean, he can always change his clothes. I'd just have wait and see what I'd have to work with.

I went straight to the bathroom figuring he'd be there before home-room. Sure enough! He was standing at the sink in front of the mirror.

 THE FIRST FORM OF MIRRORS WERE JUST SMALL POOLS OF WATER IN DARK COLORED CONTAINERS.

Not wasting any time, I launched into my attack. "Hey, Jay," I began, "Did you ever think you might . . ." I trailed off. He'd looked up at me in the mirror. His eyes were red, like he'd been crying. He *had* been crying! "Are you OK?"

Jay sniffled. "My grandma died last night," he said. "I know I haven't been your nicest friend lately. We've been worried and I haven't been sleeping well. I'm sorry, especially about yesterday. I guess I've been trying to keep everyone's attention off of me."

A sinking, guilty feeling hit the pit of my stomach. I knew I was using that verse wrong from the minute I thought about making fun of Jay. And here was the proof. I was doing the judging, not him.

Listen, I've got to work this out with Jay. Catch you later. And don't forget to flush.

YOUR TURN

- **When have you let your mood affect the way you treat other people?**
- **When have you realized too late that you were judging someone unfairly?**
- **How does it feel to be misunderstood, like Jay was?**

 SOME MIRRORS ARE MADE USING FLOAT GLASS, WATERPROOF PAINT, AND COPPER FILM.

96

I GOT DETENTION FOR SKIPPING HOMEROOM, BUT I THINK IT WAS WORTH IT.

It took exactly zero moments after I saw Jay's teary red eyes in the mirror for me to realize I was in the wrong. Just two verses after the one I was using to fuel my revenge against Jay's mild ribbing yesterday, Matthew 7:3 says, *"Why do you look at the speck of sawdust in your brother's eye and pay no attention to the plank in your own eye?"* Jesus is using *hyperbole* (hi-PER-buh-lee), a big word we learned last week in Language Arts. It means something like exaggerating nearly to the point of silliness. There's like a million reasons to use the word here: Jesus is suggesting that I've got an entire board in my eye, and I was ignoring it while trying to make fun of the flickity-fleck of dust in Jay's eye.

I realized pretty quickly that my "plank" was my own fixation on my appearance. I care about how I look, and that's fine. But I've become *so* concerned about it that when Jay pointed out a minor flaw in it—

Q: HOW MUCH CAN A PLANK WEIGH BEFORE IT TURNS INTO FISH FOOD?
A: 2,000 POUNDS. THEN IT BECOMES PLANKTON.

which actually happened to be true—I blew up and plotted biblical revenge.

I don't always get things right, but I think I did okay on this one. I apologized to Jay and confessed my intention to obliterate him with some doozy of an insult and apologized for not pausing the half second it would have taken to realize something was bugging him.

Jay pointed out that the easiest path to success would have been to make fun of him for crying and thanked me for not doing that. Kids our age can be really mean to each other, often for no reason, it seems. We agreed to try to be better friends to each other and to offer future beauty tips more subtly.

Try to find somebody to give a *compliment* to today, but try to make it about their *character*, not their appearance. And don't forget to flush.

YOUR TURN

- **How do you feel when someone attacks your character or appearance? How do you react?**
- **How often do you badger other people with casual insults?**
- **How is your faith reflected in the way you treat others?**

 TO GET ACTUAL SAWDUST OUT OF YOUR EYE, FLUSH IT WITH WATER. FROM A SINK.

97

OKAY, I HAVE JUST BLOWN MY OWN MIND. GET THIS: I AM MADE BY GOD.

That part may sound a little too easy, like a good church answer or something. It is, really. But it gets more mind blowing than that. It started in science class the other day. I love when we get to do experiments and stuff, although we haven't been able to make anything explode so far. I'm waiting for that. The other day though, Mrs. Jones let us all pair up and use these scientific balancing scales to put different weights on to observe which side went up or down. Kind of like a seesaw. Jay and I were partners and had fun stacking weights on our own side of the scale, each trying to end up the heaviest. Mrs. Jones made us quit before we were able to try adding the stacks of old textbooks to either side. She's usually pretty fun but asked if we wanted to buy the scale when it broke.

When I got home that afternoon, I kept thinking of that scale. Standing on my own scale, I realized that here at home I can only

THE MOST ANCIENT BALANCE SCALES HAVE BEEN DISCOVERED IN THE INDUS RIVER VALLEY, NEAR PAKISTAN. THEY DATE BACK TO AROUND 2000 BCE.

see my own weight and nothing really competes with it. I ended up looking up Bible verses about scales again like I did when I was trying out for wrestling. That's when I found the one that blew my mind. Proverbs 16:11 says, *"Honest scales and balances belong to the Lord; all the weights in the bag are of his making."* So when things are measured honestly, they belong to the Lord. And the weights God uses for making a fair balance are weights of God's making. Ready for the punch? So if I'm made by God, I can be a weight on the scale—helping to bring balance. That's IT! That's what blew my mind. I think that I'm made by God to balance against *injustice*. Stop and think about it. Have you ever seen that statue of Lady Justice with the blindfold and the scales of justice? I started to imagine a mini-me sitting on one side of a scale, keeping the balance fair and making sure the other side of the scale doesn't get out of whack. It's a pretty cool thought, and then you realize it must mean you've got work to do. While I'm thinking this out, don't you forget to flush, okay?

YOUR TURN

- **Have you ever had an "Aha!" moment when reading Scripture?**
- **When you realize that God's Word is giving you instructions, how does that make you feel?**
- **Imagine yourself on one side of a scale. What can you do today to help keep balance around you?**

LADY JUSTICE IS MOST COMMONLY PORTRAYED AS A BLINDFOLDED WOMAN CARRYING A SWORD AND A SET OF SCALES.

98

SINCE THAT MORNING JAY TOLD ME HIS GRANDMA HAD DIED, we've been spending a lot more time together. I told Mom and Dad about it, and Dad suggested we could go to a carnival in town, which is just about my favorite thing in the world. At some point after a lot of popcorn and cotton candy and maybe too many spinning rides, Jay and I had to go to the bathroom.

Carnival bathrooms are not amazing. *Sticky* is actually the first word that usually comes to mind. This one was unusual, though—there was some kind of old-timey scale in it that said it weighed your *personality* and then was supposed to print out a fortune. Jay was taking longer than me, and I had a quarter, so I tried it. My quarter clunked in and I stepped on. There was a winding noise and a couple of dings, then a dial spun and lights blinked wildly. The arrow stopped.

"Loser," the card read. I was a little baffled. Who would make *loser* a result on a carnival game?

  Q: WHY DON'T CARNIVAL ANIMALS EAT CARNIVAL CLOWNS?
A: THEY TASTE FUNNY.

"I don't think you're a loser." Jay had finished washing his hands and had come over to the scale.

"You don't?" I asked, a little surprised.

"Nope," he replied. "I've been doing a lot of thinking about how I treat people—not just you. I've been a little bit of a jerk sometimes. I found a verse in my grandma's Bible after she died that made me realize it. It was Proverbs 16:2: *"All a person's ways seem pure to them, but motives are weighed by the Lord."* I thought I was pretty great, but my motives were garbage. I was just looking out for myself. Tell you what, let's try this again."

He fished a quarter out of his pocket, grabbed my arm and pulled me up on the scale with him. Winding, dinging, flashing, pointing. "See?" Jay smiled. "Together, we're 'the greatest on earth.' Let's get out of here. Oh Eli—you forgot to flush."

Darn it. Make sure *you* don't forget to flush.

YOUR TURN

- **When have you realized that your behavior was selfishly motivated?**
- **Why do we usually think that we're *not* being selfish? How can you be more aware of when you are?**

 THE TILT-A-WHIRL FIRST APPEARED IN MINNESOTA AT THE 1927 STATE FAIR.

99

JAY SPENT THE NIGHT AT DAD'S WITH ME AFTER THE CARNIVAL.

The next morning, I was going in the bathroom closet to get some more toilet paper and noticed that Dad had kept his ancient avocado scale! It was like seeing an old friend. I dragged it out and put it next to the new one.

Last night Jay had borrowed Dad's Bible to show me that verse from Proverbs again, and while we had it out, I noticed another one. Proverbs 16:7 says, *"When the Lord takes pleasure in anyone's way, he causes their enemies to make peace with them."* In the last few weeks I've seen a real turnaround in the way Jay treated me, and I think I've changed a lot, too. I haven't become perfect or anything, but I feel like God is pleased with me. And Jay wasn't exactly an *enemy*, but he had certainly made peace with me lately. Things seem to be balancing out. I think I'm learning how to treat others more fairly. Justice, right?

202

  Q: HOW CAN YOU TELL THAT FISH OBSESS ABOUT THEIR WEIGHT?
A: THEY'RE SURROUNDED BY SCALES.

Oooooohhhh, balancing! I suddenly had an idea. I stepped up on both scales, one foot on each. I wiggled left and right, trying to get the same weight reading on each scale. I fell off a time or two, but kept getting back on and trying again. I was getting closer and closer to perfect—just a tenth of a pound off to the left—

"Eli."

"Yeah, Dad?"

"You realize that scale sends me a text every time you step on it, right?"

Busted. Well, I've got to go. It's been great to hang out with you for your last 99 trips to the bathroom. Maybe we'll run into each other again sometime. Until then—don't forget to flush!

YOUR TURN

- **What does _balance_ look like in your life? How do you keep your "real world" self lined up with your "spiritual self"?**
- **Who do you need to be kinder to in life?**
- **Are there people you're not even friends with that you can stick up for and show God's love to at school or somewhere else?**

203

 Q: WHAT DOES A SCALE TELL YOU WHEN YOU'RE IMPATIENT?
A: WEIGHT.

Thanks:

We'd like to thank the youth from the beach retreat years ago that planted the seed that eventually became this book:

Megan Cromer Martin, Cole Kilgo, Melissa Moore, Brandon Quarles, Jami Grayson Smith, Katie Thompson, and Shelby Williams (as best as we can recall).

We'd also like to thank the good people involved with Texas Youth Academy, whom Kevin held captive at meals for two weeks getting feedback that shaped the final proposal for this book; specifically Jon and Michelle Ashley, Katie Eichler, Eddie Erwin, Abbie Preston, Lanecia Rouse Tinsley, Ken Medema, J. Warren Smith, and Bev Vander Molen.

Most of all we'd like to thank our families and friends for their love, support, and encouragement as well as for the love and patience of our two boys, Grey and Penner, who had to read and react to each and every story, at first unwillingly and eventually for a Steph Curry jersey and a Nintendo DS. Well negotiated, boys.

K & B